FIFTY SHADES OF MARKETING

Whip Your Business Into Shape & Dominate Your Competition

Naresh Vissa

FOREWORD BY:
Philip Kotler
S. C. Johnson Distinguished Professor of International Marketing
Kellogg School of Management at Northwestern University

Thanks so much for coming to my party and for your friendship.
Good reading!

Naresh Vissa

Praise for Fifty Shades Of Marketing

"Fifty Shades Of Marketing is fifty shades of brilliant! There is way too much value here. Naresh could have charged $2,997 for it, and it would still be a bargain! What a great resource... don't start your next marketing campaign without it!"

> –Seth Greene, Bestselling author on marketing and host of the "Direct Response Marketing Magic" podcast

"The 21st century strategies and principles in Fifty Shades Of Marketing can take any person or business to the next level."

> –Jill Lublin, Former host of the TV program "Messages of Hope" and the nationally syndicated radio show "Do the Dream" and co-author of the bestselling book, "Guerrilla Publicity: Hundreds of Sure-Fire Tactics to Get Maximum Sales for Minimum Dollars"

"Here in one book, Naresh gathers and describes different tools and tactics for marketers to use in the digital age. He describes the shades of marketing with resources and his personal experiences… incorporating good stories of success with vigor and charm."

> – Philip Kotler, Founder of the World Marketing Summit and S. C. Johnson Distinguished Professor of International Marketing at the Kellogg School of Management at Northwestern University

"Fifty Shades Of Marketing has had a very measurable ROI impact on my marketing campaigns for my business CashForPurses.com. Drawing from specific strategies Naresh teaches, I was able to scale my business from 10-20 leads a day and less than $10,000 a month in revenue to over 200+ new customer leads per day with higher revenue and greater customer retention and satisfaction."

> –Trent Silver, Founder & Chief Marketing Officer of CashForPurses.com

"Fifty Shades Of Marketing is a gold mine of marketing know-how… a must read for anyone considering starting their own business. For experienced entrepreneurs, it's a refresher course on how to maximize your brand and your profits."

> –Sandy Franks, Founder & CEO of the Women's Financial Alliance

FIFTY SHADES OF MARKETING

Naresh Vissa
FIFTY SHADES OF MARKETING
Whip Your Business Into Shape & Dominate Your
Competition

ISBN-13: 978-0692554968 (Krish Publishing)
ISBN-10: 0692554963

CONTENTS

DEDICATION

To my first online marketing teachers… thank you all for introducing and showing me the ins and outs of a new industrial ecosystem.

ABOUT THE AUTHOR

Naresh Vissa is the Founder & CEO of Krish Media & Marketing – a full service online and digital media and marketing consultancy and agency. He has worked with leading publishers, media firms and corporations such as CNN Radio, JP Morgan Chase, EverBank, and Agora Publishing.

Vissa has started, shut down, taken over, quit, and sold businesses for his clients and himself. He is also the author of the #1 bestseller <u>PODCASTNOMICS: The Book Of Podcasting... To Make You Millions</u>.

Born and raised in Houston, Texas, Vissa played a lot of chess and basketball, a few instruments, and fought his way to a First Degree Black Belt in Taekwondo. He graduated Magna Cum Laude from Syracuse University's Honors Program with degrees in broadcast journalism, finance and accounting. He earned a Master's Degree from Duke University's Fuqua School of Business.

Vissa has been featured on *USA Today*, Yahoo!, Bloomberg, MSNBC, *Huffington Post*, Businessweek, *MSN Money*, *Business Insider*, *India Today*, *Hindustan Times* and other domestic and international media outlets.

Subscribe to Naresh Vissa's free mailing list at www.nareshvissa.com.

You can contact Naresh Vissa at naresh dot vissa @ gmail dot com.

FIFTY SHADES OF MARKETING

Whip Your Business Into Shape & Dominate Your Competition

FOREWORD

By Philip Kotler

Bestselling Author of over 50 Books on Marketing
Founder of the World Marketing Summit
S. C. Johnson Distinguished Professor of International Marketing
Kellogg School of Management at Northwestern University

In this book, <u>Fifty Shades Of Marketing</u>, author Naresh Vissa makes a noteworthy observation:

> "Thanks to the digital revolution, marketing has turned into a broad process."

Until the digital revolution, marketers could get along with a basic training in two broad promotional tools: advertising or sales force. Every textbook contained a chapter on each. Large companies were ready to hire you if you were up to speed on advertising or sales craft.

Today, however, you can't count on being hired with the traditional marketing training.

Naresh puts it well:

"There isn't one way to execute it [marketing]. Rather, there is a plethora of ways (or shades) to go about it."

He writes this book to illustrate *the plethora* of digital tools and marketing situations.

Today's companies expect their new marketing recruits to know many of these shades of marketing. They want to hire full-bodied digital marketers who will find one way or another to reach their target customers with a potent message and offering.

I have been a consultant to IBM, General Electric, Sony, AT&T, Bank of America, Merck, Ford, and others. Business schools around the world use my marketing materials to teach their students. My textbooks – <u>Marketing Management</u>, <u>Principles of Marketing</u>, and <u>Marketing: An Introduction</u> – have all moved to incorporate the new digital marketing. The *Financial Times* included me in its list of the top ten living business thinkers, and they cited <u>Marketing Management</u> as one of the 50 best business books of all time. These books have trained most professional marketers around the world. My readers and students gain a deep understanding of the philosophy of marketing, the key concepts and tools of marketing, the ways to build a brand, the changing marketplace, and plentiful illustrations of successful marketing and brand strategies.

FIFTY SHADES OF MARKETING

When Naresh sent <u>Fifty Shades Of Marketing</u> to me, I was impressed. Here in one book, he gathers and describes different tools and tactics for marketers to use in the digital age. Textbooks mention all of these, but Naresh goes further. He describes the shades of marketing with resources and his personal experiences... incorporating good stories of success with vigor and charm.

His book is an excellent complement to my own books. It fills a need. The guy or gal starting a new company will have a handy guide to all the digital age tools. Well-established company marketers trained before the digital age can quickly get up to speed. Those millennials who want to market their own gadget, book, or song but never had marketing training will pick up many pointers quickly. Nonprofit organizations will discover new ways to attract more museumgoers or fill seats for their performances.

I hope to see good things coming from readers who integrate the words of wisdom from Naresh's pen.

Philip Kotler
Bestselling author of more than 50 books on marketing
Founder of the World Marketing Summit
S. C. Johnson Distinguished Professor of International Marketing
Kellogg School of Management at Northwestern University
www.pkotler.org

INTRODUCTION

Every minute, hundreds of thousands of dollars are spent online… more than 200 million e-mails are sent… more than 100,000 tweets are tweeted on Twitter…

The Internet has become a necessity for the conducting of business – even brick and mortar ones. Whether it's for payments, information storage, research, or marketing, billions of people around the world are now more connected digitally than ever before… and this is just the beginning.

Every year, over 90% of businesses fail to live up to expectations – not because of the quality of their products or services, but because of their lack of execution… their inability to market themselves efficiently and effectively.

If product were king, then the *New York Times* and so many other newspapers wouldn't be going broke.

If product were king, then CHICAGO, THE HURT LOCKER, THE ARTIST, and THE KING'S SPEECH would all be in the top ten of the highest-grossing films of the millennium. None is in the top 50.

If product were king, then the highest-rated investment newsletters in *Hulbert's Digest* would have millions of paying subscribers worldwide because they generate the best investment returns. *Hulbert's Digest* provides the most proven resources to people so they have the best chance of making a lot of money through investing. Who doesn't want to make more money? Yet most investors have never heard of *Hulbert's* or its recommendations.

Good marketing is a constant for any prolific business or person. The best marketers have always been able to sustain their success. Companies like Disney and Hershey's haven't been around for a century because of their chocolates or theme parks. Remember: *It was all started by a mouse.*

Whether you're a lawyer, accountant, entrepreneur, stripper, drug dealer, or jobseeker, marketing is an important part of every single business undertaking. People need to know about you... what you offer... how you can help... why you're awesome.

In an age where nearly everything is going digital – news, music, video, radio, records, currencies, social life, and yes, even significant others – it's vital that people and companies of all kinds understand the changing environment. Say goodbye to being dependent on PCs and modems to be connected. Phones, tablets, TVs, cars, and numerous other devices now have the Internet. That's why marketing from 20 years ago no longer cuts it today.

So many successful small businesses (and large corporations) were started before the digital economy became what it is today. How we buy and what we buy is drastically different. There's been massive change, and that change has crossed over into the way businesses operate and market. Most founders and CEOs are still running their businesses – from their internal systems to their contractors and vendors – the same way they ran them when they started up shop in the 80's or 90's.

But this is the 21st century. The game has changed. Companies need to upgrade their models to a digital era. If they don't, then they're leaving money on the table.

Why Marketing's Evolution Makes It Useless In Higher Education

I didn't major in marketing in college. In grad school, I nearly failed the two marketing classes I took. One was on marketing analysis. The other was on marketing research.

In academia, most marketing classes are theoretical. They are boring. They do little to stretch the imagination.

Bookworms who learned how to conduct research in the 60's and 70's largely teach these classes. They know little about modern-day marketing applications because their research generally consists of a bunch of studies and experiments with statistical analyses. There is little useful education for guys like me who need to make money NOW.

Even though I focused my academic studies and research on finance, media and management, I never lost sight of my passion for marketing. It's something I taught myself through action and experience.

Marketing is not engineering or physics. You can't teach a marketer how to be an engineer or physicist, but you can teach an engineer or physicist how to be a marketer. You'll be surprised how good renowned engineers and physicists are at marketing. They wouldn't be renowned if they weren't.

The best marketers I know don't have PhDs or graduate degrees. They learned from the School of Hard Knocks. Anybody can be a good marketer with proper knowledge, training and experience.

I learned how to market. I paid attention to people's online and spending habits. I read about niches and how well people respond to tailored marketing. I ran my own tests and campaigns for fun during school – all of this outside the classrooms while learning about the media business and financial markets inside the classrooms.

Once I got good enough, I was hired by one of the best private marketing companies in the world right out of school to learn more, fail and succeed on my newfound passion. I was fortunate to have some of the best marketers in the world as my mentors.

Marketing evolves quickly. Every week, some new technology or strategy comes out. Marketing today is vastly different from marketing ten years ago. And ten years from now, marketing will be vastly different from what it is today.

Ten years ago, smartphones were a dime a dozen. Web design and development was a complicated and expensive process. Facebook had users in the four-figures. Twitter wasn't invented. The CAN-SPAM Act (to prevent scammers from spamming your e-mail inbox) was two years old and still open to interpretation.

Who Am I?

In this book, I've laid out principles and strategies that I have utilized, come across, or experienced. Most – if not all – of my conclusions have been formulated based on years of hands-on, nitty-gritty experience as an online and digital marketer.

I've started my own online media, marketing and publishing businesses. Some are still in business… most aren't.

I've helped start up digital media divisions for companies. Some succeeded… most failed.

I've consulted for nearly 30 different clients over the past three years. Some companies have outsourced all their marketing to me. Many clients have liked my work and still work with me. Others have cut me loose.

I've seen what works… and what doesn't (at least for me).

With failure comes lots of knowledge… and this book is a result of knowledge I've accumulated over years of failures… and some successes too.

I've written a #1 bestselling book, PODCASTNOMICS: The Book Of Podcasting… To Make You Millions. I've helped clients make millions of dollars through the content marketing medium of podcasting.

There are other marketers out there who know much more than me. How do I know that? Because I have learned from them.

I don't hold a lick to guys like Ryan Deiss from Digital Marketer and Neil Patel from KISSmetrics, but I thank them for teaching me so much about marketing through their content and conferences.

I also don't hold a lick to guys like Porter Stansberry (one of the most business-savvy publishers in the country), Brian Moran (*the* Facebook marketing guru) and Mike Palmer (the best copywriter in the world), but I'm fortunate to have worked, done business with, or learned from them in some capacity.

The Promise

I'm writing this book out of passion. I've followed marketing for years. I still have a lot to learn.

So that's why, 25 years from now, I'll rclease a sequel to this book. It'll be completely different from what it is now… not because I want it to be, but because marketing will transform again.

Nevertheless, the basic principles should be the same. Most are timeless, as you'll learn.

This book was released in 2015. If I'm alive and well, then the next version will release in 2040. I'll be in my 50's.

You can be one of the first people to find out about the sequel's release 25 years from now by subscribing to my FREE mailing list at www.nareshvissa.com. Enter your e-mail address in one of the opt-in boxes or pop-ups.

That's my promise... to prove that I'm not writing this book as a business card or to get notoriety *today*. The digital landscape is changing rapidly... and in the process, marketing is changing too. It's important that businesspeople stay on top of the transformation. I will do my best to do that because I have to... so I don't run my own businesses through the ground.

Book Structure

Thanks to the digital revolution, marketing has turned into a broad process. There isn't one way to execute it. Rather, there is a plethora of ways (or shades) to go about it.

This book has tips, tricks and resources to take you and your business to the next level through modern-day, 21st century marketing. The tips, tricks and resources are growing by the month due to increased innovation. Social networks are expanding, apps are catching on, and content publishers are multiplying.

It is my hope to help entrepreneurs and business owners better navigate the digital waters. The 20-somethings entering the world of marketing and entrepreneurship and the folks who've been marketing for decades but have fallen behind are ideal readers of this book. It's also for *anyone* who *needs* to learn **more about the online and digital world – marketers, writers, creatives and self-starters of all types**.

I've laid out strategies and principles – step-by-step – as best I can. There are more complicated techniques – such as pay per click and search engine optimization – that I recommend you hire a professional to conduct, and I walk you through how to do that. You don't have to try to implement or execute every single thing discussed. Instead, you should focus on a few that could work well for your business and try them out. See what are best, and zero in on those. If you have any questions at all or want to get more FREE tips from me, e-mail me at naresh dot vissa at gmail dot com or subscribe to my mailing list at www.nareshvissa.com.

Some areas of this book aren't as thorough as other areas in this book. This is because it's not worth walking you through every little detail. For example, it's a no-brainer that every business should have a website. But I'm not going to walk you through the process of setting up a website… not because I don't know how to do it… but rather because it would make more sense for you to hire a web designer to make a website for you.

If you'd like more information on these specific niches of marketing or want to hire an expert who can perform any of the strategies and services I discuss for you, then don't hesitate to contact me at naresh dot Vissa at gmail.com.

Feedback

If you don't agree with what I lay out in this book or think I'm dead wrong on any particular subject, then please, by all means, send me hate mail to Naresh dot Vissa at Gmail dot com... or even better, bash me up publicly by leaving a rebuttal review on Amazon or tweeting me @xnareshx.

My goal is to give people – especially marketing professionals and business owners – a full overview of the changing marketing landscape and how digital marketing can be effectively implemented into any business strategy. You, as the reader, can help accomplish this mission by communicating your thoughts and comments too by e-mailing me at Naresh dot Vissa at Gmail dot com. I plan to share good, constructive criticisms of my work or additional commentary on marketing with my mailing list subscribers. You can get on this list by visiting www.nareshvissa.com and entering your e-mail address in a newsletter opt-in box or pop-up.

Thanks for reading this book, and don't hesitate to get in touch at Naresh dot Vissa at Gmail dot com if you have any questions!

Chapter 1:
WHY DIRECT MARKETING IS THE ONLY MARKETING YOU NEED TO KNOW

I t's amazing that a majority of companies don't get *it*. It's even more surprising how many marketing, advertising and PR firms don't have a clue.

I've been in marketing for nearly ten years. I started out in marketing support (e-mail campaigns, prospecting, database management and cleansing) and then got into public and media relations, picked up social media, and finally became truly immersed with content, affiliate and direct response marketing, largely because I worked at one of the best online marketing companies in the world.

If there's one concept a manager, consultant or entrepreneur needs to learn, it's direct marketing. Even if you work in a B2B (business-to-business) setting, the principles of direct marketing still come in handy.

Direct marketing means that a business DIRECTLY CONNECTS with a consumer. How it connects is up to the business. Historically, marketers have used channels like snail mail, coupons, or telemarketing.

In today's digital ecosystem, there are more channels to directly reach a lead, potential lead, or customer. The most effective is through e-mail (like renting out mailing lists or starting an e-letter) and content (like running a blog or podcast). Other channels include social media and search (like search engine optimization, or SEO), pay per click, and targeted Facebook or Twitter (social media) ads.

Even though the players have changed, the game hasn't.

There are so many different ways to market anything, but the funnel still starts with offering something of value.

Here are a few examples that show the difference between direct response and other forms of marketing.

Example 1:

> John wants the public to know about his new bitcoin product that sells for $100. John hires a publicist for $3,500 a month. The publicist gets him on as a guest on CNN and FOX Business.

> John is happy with the exposure he's getting. His friends think he's cool because he's on TV. But when John looks at his sales the next month, he sees no spike or improvement.

The previous scenario is what so many business owners and marketers fall for. It's why the PR and branding professions are still in business.

When is the last time you watched or heard an interview on TV or in your car's radio and you said, "This author is awesome. I can't wait to go home and buy his book!" Chances are, you'll forget the guest's name, product and website within five minutes.

Example 2:

> After John's failed sales campaign through publicity, he shifts strategy. This time, he rents two different e-mail lists for $4,000 total. The lists have more than 50,000 names combined. One list is part of a gold buying website. The other list is a bitcoin blog.

> John is allowed to send one advertising message to each list – so two mailings total. He starts his emails with intrigue... subject lines like, "This Revolutionary Investment Will Protect Your Family's Assets For Generations To Come." He then teases the product in the e-mail lift, but doesn't say what it is or does. He forces readers to click a link to find out more information. The link takes readers to a "landing page" that provides all the information they need to know about the product in print and an order form at the bottom. At the top of the landing page is

also a short video clip of John talking to viewers about who he is and his new bitcoin product.

When John looks at his numbers at the end of the campaigns, he sees he got 500 new orders (less than 1% of the names he hit on the lists), which translates to $50,000 in revenue. John celebrates his returns that night at a casino.

This scenario is why direct marketing companies generally stay profitable. They're able to track data and only engage in campaigns that make sense. You probably haven't heard of these companies because they don't care about the publicity. They only focus on ROI. All the franchises within Agora Publishing, the Motley Fool and David Deangelo's dating/pick-up courses are perfect examples of businesses that effectively use direct response marketing.

Let me now give you two real-world examples…

Example 3:

Greg Smith is an ex-Goldman Sachs institutional salesman. He wrote a tell-all book about life on Wall Street, titled <u>WHY I LEFT GOLDMAN SACHS: A Wall Street Story</u>.

Smith got a big publisher, the Hachette Book Group, to market his book. It was featured in a segment on *60 Minutes* and covered in a front-page piece for the *New York Times*. Smith did interviews on all the major media outlets. He got all the publicity in the world.

Despite all the hoopla, Smith barely sold 20,000 copies of his book. He would've been lucky to make six-figures in royalties. Hachette didn't break-even on the $1.5 million advance they gave Smith.

Example 4:

James Altucher is a venture capitalist, entrepreneur and blogger. He self-published a book, <u>CHOOSE YOURSELF: Be Happy, Make Millions, Live the Dream</u>, about how people can improve their lives. Sounds stale and boring, right?

Altucher didn't go on any national media to market his book. He didn't have the backing of a traditional publisher to publicize him. Instead, he reached out to niche publications (like Tucker Max's NEW blog – not the fratire one), podcasts (Jason Hartman's *Speaking of Wealth*, which you've probably never heard of) and YouTube channels (I don't even remember the names because they have such small followings) for interviews.

He also asked his friends to write reviews of his book on their blogs and share them with their fans through social media.

One writer/publisher, Porter Stansberry, loved the book so much that he recommended it to all his readers. Stansberry sold nearly 25,000 of Altucher's books from this mention alone... and my guess is you've probably never heard of Porter Stansberry either.

Altucher made his book available for purchase through bitcoin (the largest digital currency) and offered to refund readers in total if they read his book and proved it by writing a public review.

Choose Yourself has sold more than 400,000 copies worldwide as of October 2015. Since he self-published the book and received bigger percentage cuts on sales, Altucher has now probably made seven-figures in royalties.

The preceding two examples are real. If you don't believe me, then Google the names of the books to find out for yourself. Smith's book is probably more recognizable to the public, but Altucher's book became an Amazon and *Wall Street Journal* bestseller.

Altucher found the niches. He reached out to them and asked for their help. They weren't CNBC or CNN.

Not enough companies utilize direct response online marketing. Too many corporations spend millions in advertising on TV. But TV is the idiot's medium. And idiots don't know what they're watching on TV. Idiots don't know many things.

When I visit my favorite fast food joints' websites, I find it difficult to find a newsletter or mailing list I can subscribe to. I'll be the first person to wait at a drive-thru if I have a coupon to Taco Bell. As a fast food lover, I demand that I am informed on the latest deals, offerings, changes, etc.! Otherwise, it becomes very difficult for me to know what's going on, since I don't watch TV.

The Effectiveness Of Traditional (20th Century) Ads

Write down two ads you saw in newsprint or on any website you visited over the past week. These could be ads in physical papers or magazines… or banners or space insert ads on sites.

If you remember those ads, did you visit the website being advertised, dial the call to action number, or click on the links? My estimate is that 99% of you didn't.

This exercise requires you to:

1) Remember ads after time has lapsed

2) Actually follow-up on the ads

Very few people can do both things because the ads aren't targeted. Large online media businesses can target for advertisers – like Facebook, Twitter, Google, etc. The little guy can't do this on his own.

The ads also aren't directly marketed to reach readers. They're thrown on a broadsheet and carry little meaning or thought into how they can actually help users.

Consumers Today

The world is moving towards a digital age: web, phone, tablet, etc. ComScore reported that more than 80% of the U.S. population (ages 18 and up) bought something online in the first quarter of 2014.

iAcquire reports that more than half of all online shoppers are a part of household incomes in excess of $75,000. The median household income in the U.S. is less than $50,000.

Think about the people who have access to the digital world. They spend hundreds of dollars on their devices to browse the world. It takes a qualified person to do such a thing. And there's a good chance that qualified people have more money to spend on other products and services.

This means marketers should switch from old school, brick-and-mortar strategies and instead target people on YouTube and Facebook… create a mailing list and send e-mails to subscribers… write unique content… Tweet and Instagram.

Many companies – large and small – fail to use direct response online marketing effectively. Most firms started pre-21st century operate this way. And they're keeping money on the table by doing so.

Not too many people go for "The Long Tail" when marketing anything (read Chris Anderson's book for more on that reference – it's one of the great ones written about marketing), but they should. The formula is simple: know your market… offer that market something of value (through blog posts, podcasts, e-mail, social media, etc.) … convince them that they need this product… and then at the end, "propose" an order form (or registration page, opt-in box, etc.) to them. Don't shove it in their face… nicely *propose*. Turning a consumer into a customer is a journey that needs to be nurtured gently. There's not an easier, more understandable way to put it.

> **Marketing To A Consumer** = Know your market→Offer that market something of value (through e-mail, social media, etc.)→Convince them that they need this product→"Propose"

an order form (or registration page, opt-in box, etc.)

You have to spoon-feed consumers because they're lazy. They will not buy something on their own volition unless it's a necessity. The only necessities in life are BASIC food, water, clothing, and shelter. Everything else is a luxury.

Direct marketing is – and will always be – the only way to maximize ROI. If you're a marketer or business owner, try it out for yourself.

The Unimportance Of Design

Businesses spend countless resources on things like web and logo design. Surprisingly, publisher *eMarketing & Commerce eM+C* found that poorly designed yet cluttered websites converted visitors to buyers best. Similarly, the *New York Times* reports that stores with messy and packed aisles make shoppers buy more. Visually displeasing aisles of products project greater value for shoppers. For the same reason, it's human nature to think that a store is expensive if it has very few items. That's why some of the crappiest websites have some of the highest engagement (Craigslist, Reddit, Berkshire Hathaway, Drudge Report, etc.).

A good case study is leading investment publisher Stansberry Research. Until the end of 2012, the firm didn't have a "modern-looking" website.

The site looked like it was made on MS Word 2000. I wouldn't be surprised if it was, because that's around when Stansberry was founded.

Despite the crappy-looking website, the firm made hundreds of millions of dollars over the years, solely because of its direct response marketing strategies.

I'm not saying your design should look so crappy that users barf their heads off. It actually takes skill to make something so crappy.

Only companies whose brands depend on high-quality design (like Apple) should squeal at every little minute detail. So don't stress over little things like design if that's not how your company distinguishes itself.

Going Against The Norm With Surveys

Customer surveys are stupid. They're a nag to fill out, so the responses are incredibly inaccurate.

To get precise answers, some companies offer $5-10 gift cards to individuals who fully participate. Even if customers give thoughtful answers in return, I've found the responses to be the opposite of the truth.

For example, a company I did work for sent annual surveys to its customers. Every year, customers complained about the firm's e-mail and video marketing.

"Please stop sending me so many e-mails!"

"Your videos are too long and obnoxious!"

So the company ran some tests. They segmented their mailing lists and cut down on sending so many videos and e-mails to those groups of people... the same people who said they hated videos and e-mails.

And the results were drastically worse. The people got what they wanted, but the sales numbers went down.

More marketing = more money... even if it annoys your leads and customers.

Do what makes the numbers work... not what someone suggests to improve your business on a piece of paper.

If you want to conduct a survey, make sure it's experimentally designed... meaning, create a system so you can capture the actual habits of your customers.

This is valuable data that will help you make real, impactful business decisions.

Sometimes, it's not about the content, or how the product looks, or its brand or perception. It's all about directly connecting with consumers. Of course, the product still needs to be high quality for retention, but it's even more important to get customers through the door before they buy.

Chapter 2:
WHY THE E-MAIL LIST IS THE MOST IMPORTANT ASSET A MARKETER CAN BUILD

The fastest, easiest and cheapest way to engage with your audience is by having a website with a free newsletter mailing list. Too many website owners spend energy on unique visitors, clicks, page views, etc. But none of those numbers are assets – meaning, you don't own them. They can disappear with the strike of a server.

Valuing online businesses that rely on such data becomes a challenge. For example, a few years ago, I approached one blog that seemed to be doing well. People were commenting on it, the media featured the writer a good amount, and other sites were linking back to it.

When I contacted the writer and asked what his assets were, he told me he had his web domain and brand. I did not know how to assign a dollar amount to his brand, so I asked if he had a mailing list. His response was that he got xxxx unique visitors per month.

This told me nothing about how valuable his blog actually was. So we ran banner ads on his site to see how qualified his traffic was. We got next to nothing in return.

This writer was extremely disappointed because he gave up a full-time job and spent part of his life to build his blog, and I proved to him that it was worth a little more than nothing.

My solution to him: create a mailing list to capture all that traffic. Then, advertise to that list.

This does two things:

1) Monetizes the list through advertising

2) Builds up an asset in the mailing list – the mailing list can be valued because it is tangible and quantifiable. He owned it.

The ROI on a mailing list is higher than any social media. It's better than telesales or telemarketing. It is the best way to reach your audience and make your voice heard.

Facebook announced it would start filtering promotional statuses in its News Feed. This will hurt marketers greatly. Twitter's real-time stream of information makes it easy for messages – particularly promotional ones – to get lost in the shuffle.

But an e-mail list is yours. You own it.

Facebook and Twitter can't determine what you do to your e-mail subscribers. You do. You can export the names into an Excel doc and do whatever you want with them (just don't piss them off!). You can even sell them (though that could come across as unethical if that's your only goal).

When someone opts into your list, he or she is giving you *permission* to contact him/her with more information. That trust is a golden key to a marketer.

There are entire businesses, industries, mergers and acquisitions of e-mail lists. Advertisers love spending money and running marketing campaigns to high-quality lists.

How Renting A Mailing List Helped My Last Book Become A #1 Bestseller

When I released my last book, <u>PODCASTNOMICS: The Book Of Podcasting...To Make You Millions</u>, I was disappointed with initial sales. I did a couple of Reddit AMAs, was interviewed by some small print and broadcast media, and used social media to spread the word. My book still couldn't crack 100 books sold.

Fortunately, I found a targeted blog geared towards podcasters, contacted the administrator, and asked him if I could advertise to his mailing list for nearly $300. He said very few people contacted him to advertise and that he never even thought of accepting advertising.

He agreed to my request and sent an e-mail out on my behalf to his list. He teased my book and recommended it as required reading for all podcasters.

Within 24 hours, I sold more than 90 copies of the book, and later that week, it climbed all the way to #1 in its primary category on Amazon's bestseller list. I recouped my advertising expense with that one quick and simple send.

And because it rose the charts, Amazon then started pushing my book out because they thought it would sell well moving forward... and it has.

Mailing Lists As Businesses

Countless business "publishers" do very little. They spit out horrible information and products to get people to subscribe to their free mailing lists. It sounds like a scam, but it's not, because they don't charge people to join their free mailing lists. Yet these same companies – that are such low quality – monetize their lists for six-figures in revenue a year by advertising to them.

Anyone who can grow a mailing list can get a leading company in its industry to advertise to it. For example, let's say you create a business that publishes content on organic food. To help bring in more traffic to your site, you could write content relating to organic food. You could also curate a bunch of content or find other people to guest write for you. You could then syndicate/contribute/reprint the content on several health sites and blogs to help drive traffic to your site. And then you could optimize your website so that all that traffic is being captured as leads to your mailing list or free newsletter. Once you build that list up, you could then partner with Whole Foods or Organic Valley and sell their products. They will pay you lots of money to advertise to your list! Or you could develop your own product or service and sell it to your list.

This idea applies to all businesses, not just publishers. If you're a bar owner, you could send messages to your subscribers with information on deals and coupons, special events, educational material, and more.

I once had a client who was laid off as an employee from her employer. She ran a division, and since she was let go, her division was shut down. So the company let her walk away with its assets... most notably, the mailing list. One year later, after her non-compete ended, she sold the assets to a big company for a lot of money... enough for her not to have to work for a year or two.

That's a rare example of how getting terminated from an employer can be a blessing!

I've sold mailing lists (on behalf of clients) for six-figures to private and publicly traded companies. One of these days, I might be lucky enough to procure a seven-figure sale.

It's not about web hits, Facebook Likes, or Retweets. Growing that mailing list will make your business all the more valuable!

How To Set Up Your Mailing List

When I first started e-mail marketing, I would Bcc a bunch of e-mail addresses to my Gmail account and then send out a mass blast. The first two times I did that, Gmail suspended my account for 24 hours.

The lesson I learned: do not add a bunch of names to your Gmail and e-mail them. That is the worst way to send a message to a mass audience.

Gmail only allows you to send to 250 recipients at a time. If Gmail detects bulk sending, then it will shut down your e-mail account for 24 hours and future messages may be marked as spam.

Mailing List Resource

www.MailChimp.com

MailChimp is quickly becoming the most common e-mail service provider (ESP). The company has become a household name because of its smart decision to advertise on the first mainstream and most listened to podcast of all time, *Serial*. I use MailChimp for my businesses and love its features. It's also very cheap compared to competitors like AWeber, Constant Contact, iContact and Infusionsoft.

MailChimp allows you to import a spreadsheet of existing e-mails if you already have them, and it will even cleanse your list to get rid of any bad e-mails. This will reduce the chances of your domain being shut down or your "From" e-mail address being marked as spam.

Once you get your ESP set up, you can connect it to your website so that you can capture names. See your ESP's FAQs on how you can do this… or better yet, hire a web designer or developer overseas for $10 at www.upwork.com (formerly Elance/oDesk) so he can do all this for you smoothly.

How To Optimize Your Website And Capture Names To Grow Your List

To capture names, make sure you have plenty of newsletter opt-in boxes and maybe even a pop-up asking visitors to subscribe to your free mailing list so they can stay up to date on your latest deals, special events, content, and other goodies.

Coming up are some images that explain what I mean. The screenshots are taken from one of my research firms, *Moneyball Economics*.

Example of a pop-up:

Example of an opt-in box:

I've had clients force users to enter their e-mail address in order to browse around the site or get something of value. Take this example from a podcast client: When visitors click the "Play" button or "Listen" for a podcast, a pop-up comes up immediately asking the user to enter their e-mail into a box so they can listen to the episode they clicked on. The only way they can listen to the podcast would be by entering their e-mail address. This seems forceful, but it's a great way to collect new e-mail leads.

Going back to the bar owner example from earlier in this chapter... you could post coupons on your site. Once users click them to download, a pop-up comes up asking them to enter their e-mail address so the coupon can be e-mailed to them.

THE QUICKEST WAY TO GROW YOUR MAILING LIST IS TO "GIVE AWAY" SOMETHING OF VALUE FREE OF CHARGE. Here are examples of what businesses can give away to their sites' visitors free of charge:

- Special report

- E-book

- Special audio or video interview

- One-year free trial to a product

- Free consultation

- Coupon or discount code

You want to highlight your giveaway as much as possible. The copy should clearly say what you're giving away, why it's of value, and how people can take advantage of this offer (i.e. "Enter Your E-mai" Address Below To Get Your FREE XYZ").

For one former podcast client of mine, I ran a campaign where we gave away free digital subscriptions to a paid newsletter if people entered their e-mail on a landing page we created on a vanity URL. We plugged the URL on-air during the podcasts. We built our mailing list to more than 10,000 subscribers from scratch over a one-month period because of this campaign.

You can easily fulfill the "giveaway" through an autoresponder e-mail within your ESP... just search for the "Autoresponder" section of your ESP to set it up.

Going back to the bar hypothetical... a bar owner could give customers a questionnaire, and in return for filling it out (with their e-mail address listed), they received a free pizza slice or beer or shot of Tequila.

I'm thinking of ideas off the top of my head and sharing them. The point is to get YOU to start thinking about how you can apply these principles to your own business.

How To Grow Your List If You Already Have Customers

I once had a client who had more than 2,000 clients. He grew his business in a traditional, man-to-man fashion. He asked me how he could better cross-promote his products and services.

I told him to get the e-mails of all his clients and put them in a mailing list. He could do this because he had to get approval to perform services or file paperwork for his clients every year. So he didn't have to go out of his way to get e-mails. He also had two assistants working for him, so he didn't have to spend any additional time to collect this information.

The mailing list changed his business dramatically. Gone were the days of hunting down clients on the phone to communicate or cross-promote them.

What To Send To Your Mailing List

Whatever new content you post on your site, also send it through your mailing list, and vice-versa. Posting content on your site leaves the door open for something to go viral. It improves SEO.

Sending a message to your mailing list directly reaches your subscribers. They don't need to go searching on your website for your information. Mailings are instant and time-sensitive notices that show up in people's inboxes.

In your e-mail templates, make sure you include a link to the original piece on the website. That way, if someone forwards your e-mail to a friend, the friend can click that link and join your mailing list. Or he share the link with his friends, thus driving mo to your site and increasing the chances of growing your list.

In the example, you'll notice the circled text says, "Read this article on the *Moneyball Economics* website by clicking here."

If you're sending out a sales e-mail to take orders on a product or collect leads externally through an affiliate, then make sure your hyperlinks go to one page only. You don't want to forward readers to different places. All the hyperlinks must go to the same page. The focus should be on one page and one page only.

Many e-mail marketers make the mistake of saving the call to action or hyperlink until the end of the e-mail message.

They'll end with something like, "Click here to find out more."

Instead, try to incorporate hyperlinks at the beginning, middle and end of the e-mail, at the very least.

Hyperlink to that page throughout your e-mail copy. There should be a minimum of three hyperlinks within your e-mail. The more hyperlinks in your sales message, the greater the likelihood the reader clicks one of those links.

For editorial e-mail sends (like sending your blog content, which will be discussed later in the book), sales are irrelevant, so you can hyperlink to whatever makes sense in the editorial.

How Split Testing Will Get You Great E-mail Marketing Results

Suppose you're selling a product, and you have drafted three pieces of e-mail copy lifts. If you want to see which of the three performs best, then send out each piece of copy to your list in 5% segments. In other words, if you have 10,000 people on your mailing list, then send 500 (5% of 10,000 people) people Copy 1, a new set of 500 people Copy 2, and another new set of 500 people Copy 3. After all these *tests*, you can see which performs best and use it to blast the entire list. You'll know exactly what works best… not just the copy, but also the subject line, landing page, etc.

Best Days And Times To Send E-mails To Your List

There are all sorts of combinations that researchers have published on when to send e-mails. Over the years, I've tested it all. This is what I found:

Tuesdays, Wednesdays and Thursdays between 8:00-9:00am ET and 3:30-4:30pm ET are the best days and times to send mass e-mails.

Let's now think about why these times make sense, and why the other days and times *don't* make sense...

E-mails are most effective within one hour after they're sent. The longer time passes, the more shine an e-mail loses.

Most people are getting ready for work or getting their children ready for school before 8am ET, so they won't have time to be at their computers. When workers enter their office – sometime between 8:00 and 9:00am ET – the first thing they'll likely do is check their e-mails and catch up on news.

The same theory can be applied after 5pm ET. Again, people will leave work for the day around 5pm ET sharp. The last things they'll want to do for the rest of the day is do work or check their e-mails. That's why the last full hour of work – 3:30-4:30pm ET – is a great timeframe to blast a mailing list.

Let's now think why these days (Tuesday, Wednesday, Thursday) make sense...

Monday is the first working day back from the weekend. It's generally the busiest day of the week because workers set up meetings to get their action items in order. Therefore, e-mails can be missed on Mondays.

People tend to get lazy on Fridays because they're looking forward to the weekend. Some companies give their employees Fridays off. Others give them half-days. Therefore, Friday's are terrible days to send mass e-mails.

Furthermore, holidays (inside and outside the U.S.) tend to fall on Mondays and Fridays. So not sending e-mail on these days will prevent you from accidentally sending something on these days (this sentence sounds dumb, but one time, I accidentally sent a mass e-mail on Columbus Day and got zero response).

Very few people work on weekends. E-mailing on a Sunday, especially if it's a sales message, even offends some people. So don't e-mail on weekends.

Since it's so important, I'll write it again:

Tuesdays, Wednesdays and Thursdays between 8:00-9:00am ET and 4:00-5:00pm ET are the best days and times to send mass e-mails.

How Frequently Can You Message Your List?

There's a misconception that sending too many messages will dilute your list. That is false.

Of all people, Barack Obama and his 2012 presidential campaign proved that more e-mail sends do not equate to more unsubscribes. I tested this tactic when I was running a division for a former employer. We increased our sending volume times four. Our revenue went up eight-fold.

More marketing sends = more return.

You don't want to hit your list more than twice a day (over a five-day working week). You also want to send to your list at least twice a month.

Consider this equation that helps put send frequency in an algebraic format:

2 sends per month < x < 2 sends per day (over a five-day working week)

Where x is the number of e-mails you send

Don't abuse your list… but don't be afraid to hit it.

If you send a mass e-mail and want to know how quickly you'll start seeing some results, then follow the 24-Hour Rule. Popular sales blog *Yesware* found that an e-mail loses its gleam after 24 hours.

So if you send a sales e-mail at 8am ET on a Tuesday, and you don't get any responses by 8am ET on the next day (Wednesday), then that means your campaign failed. You may get a couple of responses in the future, but generally, e-mails get lost in the shuffle 24 hours after they're sent. It would be a good idea to send another e-mail with a different message and copy.

Chapter 3:
HOW AFFILIATE MARKETING CAN GENERATE REVENUE RAPIDLY WITH VERY LITTLE WORK

Imagine you're a businessperson. You have a great product or service. Now, you need to go to market. But you can't afford to spend a ton of money on unproven or risky marketing.

Affiliate marketing is referral marketing. It is the safest and most efficient way to grow a business. You get other people to refer you (affiliates), and in return, they get commissions (or some other token of appreciation) for each referral.

Not everyone a company pays makes the firm money. Many of these people are deadweight.

With affiliate marketing, you are paying people or companies because they are making you money. That's the best way to conduct business.

Let's say you're a lawyer and you start your own practice. You need clients. You could spend a lot of money and time on classified ads, social media, blogging, podcasting, and other digital strategies to bring in clientele.

Or you could go the affiliate route...

You call all your friends and family and tell them tell them that if they refer a friend to you, then they (the referrer) will get $1,000 worth of free legal counsel or services (about three billable legal hours). $1000 can be a lot of money for most people.

To entice new customers, you can give them a free consultation or 25% off the first $1,000 they spend in legal services.

A deal like this doesn't cost you anything out of pocket – unlike paying thousands of dollars on pay per click or social media ads. And it gives the referrer (affiliate) a big incentive to forward you referrals.

So you let everyone know about your affiliate referral program: friends, family, homeless people on the street (they need legal services too!), and most importantly, your clients and customers – old and new.

Your customers are always your best marketers. They have mouths that make noises. They have relationships with real people. They express their thoughts on the Internet and digital world so that you don't have to.

Before you know it, you'll have new customers coming for your help. You can then hire more employees (or temporary workers or contractors) to fulfill all the work that needs to be done.

Why Customer Lifetime Value Is The Most Important Metric Marketers Need To Know

Now, let's say you're a techpreneur. You invented a widget that sells for $100.

You start an affiliate program. You tell your friends and family to sell the widget for you. You also reach out to other tech companies and publishers to sell your product. Everyone is given uniquely coded links they need to use, publicize and market so their respective referrals can be tracked.

Resource: use Mixpanel (www.mixpanel.com) to create and track uniquely coded links for affiliates.

The question now shifts from, "How do I market my product?" to "How much do I pay people to market my product?" The amount you pay has to be enticing enough for other people to market you. If you don't offer enough in return, then nobody will want to plug you.

Customer lifetime value (CLV) is the total dollar value of a customer over the life of his or her relationship with a business.

So in your case, if a customer buys your $100 widget and then never buys anything from you again, then their CLV is $100.

If they buy your $100 widget, and then buy a $50 complement to your widget, and then buy a newer version of your $100 widget three years later, and then they die in a car accident, then their CLV is $250 ($100 widget + $50 complement + $100 widget three years later).

Most people think they should pay their affiliates a cut of the sale they make. In this case, this means you'd give your affiliates a cut of your $100 widget. That can work, but again, if your offer to them is low, then they won't feel the need to sell your product.

But once you calculate your customer lifetime value, which will usually be greater than a point of sale, the numbers will support you in offering more money to your affiliates.

That's why AT&T and Apple give away $1 iPhones... because they can afford to lose money on the phone because users will end up spending hundreds of dollars on data plans, monthly subscriptions, case covers, chargers, apps, and other complements over the course of many years. The phone set acts as a loss leader to funnel customers into buying other products and services. Its cost to the companies is sunk.

Note: The CLV could be less than a point of sale if a company sells multiple products at vastly different price points. For example, a subscription business can have a $50/year (front-end) product and a $5,000/year (back-end) product. Because a majority of the people will go for the $50/year product, the CLV for the company will be far less than the $5000 amount on one back-end product.

How To Calculate Customer Lifetime Value

I've written a whole section on the importance of finding your customer lifetime vale. The only problem is that calculating your CLV is not easy.

There are multiple ways to do it. No way has proven to be right or wrong. Mathematicians or statisticians would be able to undertake such a long and complicated process.

Here are the easiest ways to break it down:

Customer Lifetime Value of a Frequent Customer (grocery shopper, magazine subscriber, cable or Internet subscriber, etc.) = (Average Monthly Revenue per Customer * Gross Margin per Customer) / Monthly Churn Rate

Customer Lifetime Value of a Long-term Customer (legal or accounting client, software buyer, car buyer, etc.) = (Average Annual Revenue per Customer * Gross Margin per Customer) / Annual Churn Rate

The churn rate is the percentage of customers who end their relationship with you in a given period. One minus the churn rate is the retention rate.

Your retention rate = 1-churn rate.

This is a lot of math. I likely lost most of you. I get lost looking at these equations. So here are the important takeaways that improve customer lifetime value:

- Keep your customers

- Upsell your customers higher-priced products or services

You can hire a math or statistics PhD student for $1,000 as a one-week contractor to calculate your firm's customer lifetime value.

Or, for a quick, simple, and free calculation, visit www.customerlifetimevalue.co and enter the key data they ask for. This is a free CLV calculator, so you'll get what you pay for.

Using Customer Lifetime Value In Affiliate Marketing

Once you know your customer lifetime value, you can start offering better deals to your affiliates.

Going back to the widget example earlier in this chapter...

If the CLV of your tech company is $200, and your widget still costs $100, then you can pay your affiliates more than the cost of the product (like $110 or $120) and still make money.

Can you imagine being an affiliate and referring people to buy a $100 product, yet you're getting paid $110 in return for that simple referral? You'd actually think you're making more money than the firm is!

What a steal...

This is what makes affiliate marketing a meaningful exercise... leading to enormous profits with very little work.

Affiliate Marketing Resources

www.similarsites.com – allows users to search for and research potential affiliates in your niche. Just type in your website (or a larger competitor's), and out will come a bunch of similar sites who can be your potential affiliates.

Mixpanel (www.mixpanel.com) is becoming a go-to analytics platform for online marketers. It offers a variety of free and paid products and services, one of which is creating affiliate links and tracking clicks, orders, leads and referrals.

ClickBank (www.clickbank.com) is the most popular affiliate marketing outlet because it's been around since the late 90's, but Mixpanel (founded in 2009) is quickly making up ground and offering more features in an easy-to-use fashion.

Nanacast (www.nanacast.com) is an integrated online shopping cart that includes full affiliate services, instant revenue sharing, and one-click upsells. It is compatible with all e-mail service providers.

www.customerlifetimevalue.co – free customer lifetime value calculator

Chapter 4:
WHY MARKET TESTING IS SO IMPORTANT

Every marketer, designer, and copywriter will run into a very good problem to have...

They'll come out with multiple mock-ups... not just *the one*.

Marketers will generate lots of ideas. Designers will create many designs. Copywriters will formulate different versions of copy. Advertisers and branders will concoct various slogans.

So what's the best way to pick what's right?

Test them all out...

If you want to see which of three banners performs best, then test each banner for a week on your website and see which banner generates the most click-throughs. This is the only way to use your full ROI potential... to put your best foot forward.

If you want to see which of the three pieces of e-mail copy performs best, then send out each piece of copy to your list in 5% segments. In other words, if you have 10,000 people on your mailing list, then send 500 (5%

of 10,000 people) people Copy 1, a new set of 500 people Copy 2, and another new set of 500 people Copy 3. After all these *tests*, you can see which performs best and use it to blast the entire list. You'll know exactly what works best… not just the body copy, but also the subject line, landing page, etc.

If you're a national sandwich chain, you can test slogans in different markets. Come out with five different slogans and test each one in five different states. Then, at the end, look at the data to see which was most effective.

I've been very surprised to see data prove me wrong countless times. It's easy for marketers like me to fall in love with themselves. They may think one way is the best way.

Testing and letting the numbers do the talking are the only ways to ensure you're maximizing your marketing resources.

Why Customer Surveys Aren't Good Testing Controls

Customer surveys are stupid. They're a nag to fill out, so the responses are incredibly inaccurate.

To get precise answers, some companies offer $5-10 gift cards to individuals who fully participate. Even if customers give thoughtful answers in return, I've found the responses to be the opposite of the truth.

For example, a company I worked at sent annual surveys to its customers. Every year, customers complained about the firm's e-mail and video marketing.

"Please stop sending me so many e-mails!"

"Your videos are too long and obnoxious!"

So the company ran some tests. They segmented their mailing lists and cut down on sending so many videos and e-mails to these groups of people... the same people who said they hated videos and e-mails.

The results were drastically worse. People got what they wanted, but the sales numbers went down.

More marketing = more money... even if it annoys your leads and customers.

Do what makes the numbers work... not what someone suggests to improve your business on a piece of paper.

If you want to conduct a survey, make sure it's experimentally designed... meaning, create a system so you can capture the actual habits of your customers. This is valuable data that will help you make real, impactful business decisions.

Chapter 5:
WHY PPC ADVERTISING IS BETTER THAN CPM ADVERTISING

Google was the first big company to introduce a brand new form of online advertising for publishers and advertisers to test in a multitude of ways.

Now, most social networks sites that monetize off advertising quantify ad spend through PPC (pay per click) and CPM (cost per thousand) metrics without getting Google involved. They run their own advertising programs.

For advertisers, pay per click advertising is recommended over cost per thousand advertising. Here's why...

CPM advertisers generally pay on a historical average per thousand views. For example, if a site gets 2,000 hits a month, and if an advertiser wants to advertise a banner on the site and pays a CPM (cost per thousand) of $50, then that means the advertiser will pay $100 to advertise a banner on this site ($50 per thousand hits means $100 per 2,000 hits. The algebraic equation to solve this would be $50/1,000 hits = $x/2,000 hits. Solving for x gets you $100.)

Advertisers pay for what they get in PPC. The more clicks you get (which is what you want), the more you pay. The fewer the clicks, the less you pay. All parties win.

With CPM, there's no telling what you'll get in return. You could pay a lump sum up front and get nothing back.

Additionally, ad-blocking software has curbed the visibility of web advertising. Ad blockers keep users from viewing ads. This means CPM advertisers stand to be paying for traffic that they won't even be receiving. This is a huge waste of advertising dollars!

Advertising Resource

www.whatrunswhere.com is a good subscription service that provides detailed intelligence on what and where your competition is advertising. You can copy what's working for them and stay away from places where their campaigns have failed. This is the closest thing to buying inside information on your competition!

Why Marketers Should Outsource Google AdWords

Google AdWords is a service that places advertising copy around Google search results. AdWords users can target the search terms where their advertising will show up. They can also target search engine searchers who search by location – specific countries, regions, cities, zip codes, etc. The platform can target searchers based on where they are and what they browse.

AdWords users pay per click (PPC) on their advertisement. This pay-for-performance structure means AdWords users and Google have a high likelihood of making money together.

AdWords has become so popular to online marketers that Google makes billions of dollars off this service. It is now Google's main source of profit because its margins are so thin and therefore can run in an automated and scalable fashion.

With all that being said, I don't suggest fledgling or novice marketers try Google AdWords. If you don't run your campaigns properly, then it's very easy for bad traffic to click the ads... meaning you won't see much return and your tab will be run up. I had to learn this the hard way, and it's why I now outsource AdWords campaigns to professionals for my clients and personal projects.

To make AdWords most effective, you need to outbid your competition for ad spaces. Companies that spend tens of thousands of dollars on AdWords have a much better chance of seeing a return than a little guy like me spending a few hundred bucks. There's no way a small player can compete with big dawgs with deep pockets.

Compared to other forms of marketing, AdWords is very expensive – even though it does have the potential to get you a greater return more quickly.

If you have the money and want to get aggressive with your marketing, then give AdWords a shot… but hire an expert to handle your campaigns. SEO and PPC veterans are worth the cost because their experience will be saving you much time and heartache.

Need Help With Google AdWords?

Contact me at naresh dot Vissa at Gmail dot com if you're in need of an AdWords expert who can help your efforts. I know some of the best independent AdWords managers in the world and would be glad to make connections. They've generated tens of millions of dollars for some very successful online marketers and publishers.

Successful AdWords campaigns have the potential to jumpstart your business into the forefront and generate profits for lifetimes.

2 Alternative Ways To Market Using Google

Google+ is Google's prime social network. Google also owns YouTube. It's the second largest search engine in the world (after its parent Google). This means that both Google+ and YouTube have high search engine optimization (since Google will make sure they're at the top of search results).

What does this mean to you? It means you should:

1) **Post your videos on YouTube**. It's the second largest site in the world. If your content is good, people will find it.

2) **Create Google+ accounts for you and your businesses.** Post all relevant information on Google+. Run the account like you would your Facebook or Twitter accounts. If you're an online writer or blogger, post your articles to your account. Google+ will show up at the top of search results with your profile picture and description/bio, so make sure you highlight your strengths to maximize the exposure you're getting.

Resource & AdWords Alternative: Yahoo Gemini

Yahoo Gemini's platform is sort of like Google AdWords. However, campaigns are easier to create and run. Therefore, I'd recommend Gemini for beginner or novice Internet marketers.

Unlike Google and Amazon, Yahoo is not known for its customer service. This means you'll get very little guidance in managing your account, unless you spend tens of thousands of dollars. So with Yahoo Gemini, you're pretty much on your own. Customer service won't talk to you on the phone, and they won't respond to your e-mails either.

Similar to AdWords, you'll truly get a great return on your Gemini spend if you open up your wallet and spend a lot of money.

Pay Per Click Wrap-up

To summarize, companies or individuals should keep the following ideas for Google AdWords or Yahoo Gemini pay-per-click campaigns in mind:

1) You have five-figures to spend on advertising.

2) You know a pay-per-click expert who can run campaigns for them (contact me at Naresh dot Vissa at Gmail dot com to be introduced to some of the best).

Chapter 6:
WHY MOBILE IS THE FUTURE OF MARKETING

I talk repeatedly in this book about how mobile marketing isn't proven... yet. People still aren't used to buying lots of stuff on their handsets.

Nevertheless, mobile is something all companies should be paying attention to. And in the future, it'll be the most prominent channel to market to... because people won't be using PCs or laptops as much, according to Gartner. PCs (desktops and notebooks) are dying. Tablet sales are steadily rising.

Television is dying. Radio is dying. Print media is dying. But smartphone adoption is rapidly picking up domestically. The percentage of smartphone owners (as a share of total mobile users) rose from about 40% past 70% in a matter of three years (2012-2014), according to a comScore study.

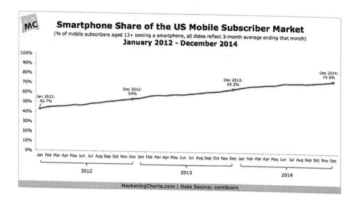

Marketing Land found people to spend more time on their phones than any other media, including TV. By the end of 2018, Statista forecasts there will be 220 million smartphone users. There are nearly 320 million people in the U.S. This means that approximately 70% of the country will own a smartphone such as an iPhone or Android.

That's a huge percentage of the population who will have access to their e-mail, apps, Internet, and other tidbits on their phones. The old flip phones are now irrelevant.

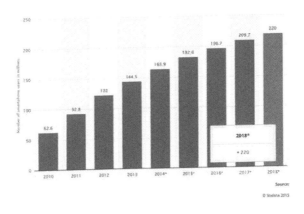

Emerging markets like India and China have populations much greater than the United States has. And smartphones are quickly catching on there too, in addition to numerous other international markets.

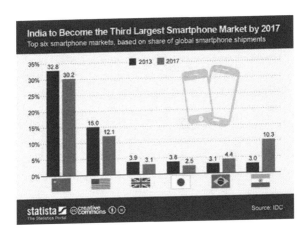

Telecommunication giants and phone makers are "giving away" phones for free (or close to it) with fixed-term contracts to escalate growth. Given how much people are now spending on their phone plans –

with unlimited texting and more-than-enough data to surf the net and use other cool apps at a little over $50 per month – it only makes sense for continued adoption.

Due to the massive progress in mobile, an entire industry worth trillions of dollars has burgeoned. Some mobile-dependent applications – like photo messaging network Snapchat and ridesharing service Uber – have valuations above $25 billion each. Dating apps like Tinder and Coffee Meets Bagel have helped people find love (or at least get laid).

And complementary products to mobile – such as payment processors, Bluetooth devices, and smartwatches – are creating another new industry that is growing.

As people get more comfortable with their smartphones, and as developers improve the ease of use, mobile will be where business is done. Already, payments, banking, dating, communication, networking, art, writing, recording, and more are on mobile platforms.

Millennials Will Be The Buyers... On Mobile Devices

The digital age has coincided with millennial maturation. Millennial men don't want to shop at department or grocery stores anymore. Retails shop customers are slowly becoming predominantly female.

Bank branches have less millennial customers visiting them because millennials would rather deposit their checks or make changes to their accounts online or through their mobile phones.

Millennials are rapidly moving money through payment processors like Square and payment transmitters like PayPal and Venmo. The big banks are also improving their own applications to improve commerce, which millennials are making use of.

Spanish is the second most spoken language in the United States. Media Metrix Multi-Platform found that two out of every five millennials of Spanish-speaking origin are "mobile-only" users – meaning they don't use computers or tablets for anything. They conduct all their business – reading, communicating, and working – on their phones.

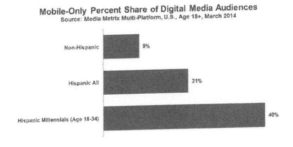

Mobile-Only Percent Share of Digital Media Audiences
Source: Media Metrix Multi-Platform, U.S., Age 18+, March 2014

Non-Hispanic	9%
Hispanic All	21%
Hispanic Millennials (Age 18-34)	40%

Media Metrix Multi-Platform found that one out of every five American millennials is "mobile-only."

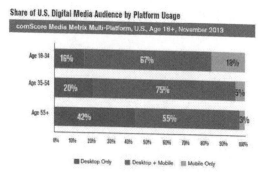

ComScore Mobilens reports that the adoption of smartphones among millennials has surpassed any other age class. This is despite millennials not having as much money in the bank as their older counterparts, who are more likely to afford intricate smartphones and their data plans.

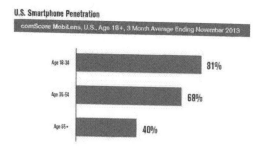

Millennials have grown up in a changing – and improving – technological environment. The Internet and PCs were big in the 90's, and then iPods and laptops ruled the first decade of the 2000's. Now, tablets and mobile are dominating the second decade of the 2000's. That's why millennials are quick adopters and better adapters. There wasn't so much technological change during the Baby Boomer days.

So What Does The Mobile Explosion Mean For Businesses?

To start, it means all businesses should make sure their sites, products and features and optimized for mobile. A clunky or discombobulated site on mobile will result in a high bounce rate.

Eventually, *everything* will find a way to mobile. Over the long-term, it won't be necessary to sit in front of a computer to waste time. It won't be necessary to have an office phone. In fact, it won't even be necessary to go into an office to work.

Approximately 40% of all e-mail is viewed via smartphones and tablets today. If 40% of people are getting their messages through these channels, then you MUST find ways to not only optimize your sites to mobile, but also tailor your e-mails and sales messages in such a way to entice these specific users. If your company needs the highest quality and most up-to-date mobile marketing /advertising services, then contact me at Naresh dot Vissa at Gmail dot com, and I'll refer you to the very best of the best.

Another takeaway is that ads need to be optimized for mobile. For example, *Mobile Marketer* found that 970x250 banners are great for desktops and laptops, but 320x50 work best on smartphones and tablets.

Nielsen reported that mobile APPLICATIONS (apps) now account for 90% of all time users spend on their smartphones. Mobile ad tracking firm Medialets found that advertisements in mobile apps perform significantly better (0.56% click-through rates) than ads on the mobile web (0.23% click-through rates). The click-through rates aren't as high as they would be for e-mail advertisements, but the data nonetheless is an encouraging sign for mobile advertisers moving forward.

Some large brands are already testing ad campaigns on mobile applications. For example, during Valentine's 2014, Domino's in the United Kingdom used dating app Tinder to reach users. Anyone who matched with the Domino's Tinder account had the opportunity to get a discounted pizza.

Consumer Intelligence Research Partners (CIRP) also found Facebook to be the most used mobile app. This presents a tremendous advertising opportunity within Facebook.

It's important that all businesses – including brick-and-mortar, man-to-man shops – keep the mobile trend in mind for the future. Those who adapt to these changes will be ahead of the curve.

Why Mobile Apps For Small Businesses Are Not Proven Marketing Vehicles

The mobile app space is such a cutthroat industry. Why? Think about the apps you have on your phone. No person is going to download every app they come across. People only use the apps they need. Within that set of apps, they'll concentrate again only on a select few apps. And to save space, they'll delete whatever they don't need.

App advertising firm Flurry Analytics reported that mobile users use apps at the same rate today (8.8) as they did four years ago (8.9).

That's why the mobile app space is dominated by big players: large companies and brands who convert their existing customers to their app – such as Facebook, Twitter, LinkedIn, Spotify, Pandora, Yelp, Google Maps/Chrome, Bloomberg, and big commercial banks… or mobile app companies that distinguished themselves from the pack to gain market share – start-ups like Snapchat, Instagram, Uber, Lyft, Tinder, Coffee Meets Bagel, Hinge, Robinhood, GroupMe, and Venmo.

It's very difficult to make it as a small player in the mobile app space. I know of countless individuals who raised and spent lots of money to create mobile apps. With the exception of a friend of a friend who hit it big with one of the companies I named, every single one of the apps failed.

Flurry also found that more than half of all apps lose more than half of their users within three months of reaching their peak number of monthly active users (MAU). This means that retention is incredibly low within the app space.

Mobile Apps Are Pricy

Development can be very expensive for intricate apps. So many start-up apps fail because they run out of funding.

Business Insider found that frequent app updates correlate to higher ratings. Higher ratings mean better optimization in the respective App Store (for both Google and Android). So app development is a drawn out process. Apps need constant tweaking and upgrading, so you'll have to have a developer on retainer at all times after you launch your beta version. The base cost for such services is in the hundreds of thousands of dollars.

So What Do Mobile Apps Mean For Existing Businesses?

Only release an app if you have an existing customer base who you can convert into app users. I shared examples earlier... companies like Facebook, Pandora, and Bloomberg did this. They started out as pre-mobile businesses and offered something completely different but then added the apps to their repertoire.

So if you're a growing business with customers, an app is something you may want to think about. A mobile app would keep users updated on your business, deals, and other tidbits. You can outsource this overseas... go to www.upwork.com (formerly Elance/oDesk) to find the most reasonable prices.

Once you have an app and a strong user base, your "app list" becomes incredibly valuable. You can send users in-app messages with deals and offers for quick conversion. You'll also capture users' e-mail addresses when they download the app, so you can communicate with them via e-mail too.

Mobile App Advertising

Mobile advertising is still trying to figure itself out. People aren't used to purchasing or doing major work on their phones or tablets yet. Therefore, mobile advertising costs are sky high.

Nielsen reported that mobile APPLICATIONS (apps) now account for 90% of all time users spend on their smartphones. Mobile ad tracking firm Medialets found that advertisements in mobile applications perform significantly better (0.56% click-through rates) than ads on the mobile web (0.23% click-through rates). The click-through rates aren't as high as they would be for e-mail advertisements, but the data nonetheless is an encouraging sign for mobile advertisers moving forward.

Big corporations – like Domino's Pizza – are dabbling and testing. During Valentine's 2014, Domino's in the United Kingdom used dating app Tinder to reach users. Anyone who matched with the Domino's Tinder account had the opportunity to get a discounted pizza. More brands are testing similar campaigns.

E-mail marketing is cheaper and much more proven. Until there's further clarity on how reactive mobile advertising is, it would be best for smaller businesses to keep away from it.

Chapter 7:
HOW SOCIAL MEDIA IMPROVES BRANDING... BUT DOES LITTLE FOR ROI MARKETING

W ord of mouth is the most powerful marketing known to man. It's how marketing was invented centuries ago. That's why customers are the best marketers on the planet.

Combine this idea with the fact that so many people live on their Twitter feeds, Facebook Timelines, and Instagrams, and you'd think that social media should be the one-stop shop for e-commerce.

But an IBM report found that 0.68% of online sales on Black Friday 2012 came from Facebook referrals. For all the shopping that's done online, that's close to nothing.

The same report found that 0% of online sales on Black Friday 2012 came from Twitter referrals. *That is nothing...* not close to nothing or next to nothing... but *absolutely nothing.* Twitter's real-time stream of information makes it easy for messages – particularly promotional ones – to get lost in the shuffle.

Social media is *social...* not promotional. The social media industry was created so that friends could stay in touch and get to know each other. People don't like being sold to on social media. And they don't like other social accounts that brag about themselves and their accomplishments.

That's why Facebook announced it would start filtering promotional statuses in its News Feed. This is going to hurt ROI marketers greatly.

Consequently, social media is more a *branding* tool than a moneymaking channel. Every business *needs* to have *a presence* on social media. *Presence* doesn't mean just having accounts and pages. It means pumping out regular statuses, posts and updates. These are now requirements. Social media presence keeps the door open to being discovered through a variety of markets.

Not having a presence will lose you Gen Y. For millennials, viewing a brand through digital media holds more strength than viewing a brand on a billboard or in a magazine.

4 Important Social Media Takeaways

1) **Being active on social media is necessary, but don't take your paid marketing efforts on them too seriously.**

Build followings on social media so people can share your content with their networks. Post your content (depending on the form) on YouTube, Facebook, Twitter, Myspace, Pinterest, etc.

Give your audience of followers what they want. Post updates and respond to public and private messages. Do whatever you need to do to stay active and engaged on social media.

Congratulate loyal social media followers publicly. Your audience will get a kick out of it. It'll convey a sense of realness.

Social media has real *intangible* value. Social media won't make you rich, but it'll increase your brand, awareness and engagement greatly. It's awesome for customer service. It also leaves several doors open for virality. These days, nothing can go viral without social media.

2) **The key to social media engagement: enticing headlines.**

People judge content by their headlines like people judge books by their front covers. So make your 140 characters on Twitter count. Make people *want* to click on what you post.

In general, numbers in headlines are good – i.e. "4 Ways To Improve Your Life", "10 Hacks To Get Free Airline Tickets", etc.

"How To" is also a great way to start a headline – i.e. "How To Get A Girlfriend", "How To Eat A Triple Pound Hotdog", etc.

3) **Respond to public and private questions and comments.**

Tweets, retweets, mentions, replies, comments, comments within comments, direct messages, private messages… respond to them if they're questions or compliments. It shows there's someone behind your brand and that you don't have a robot running your accounts.

You may not want to respond to everything you get because some things aren't worth responding to (insults, divisive statements or topics, content that crosses legal lines).

4) **RESOURCE:** Hootsuite **(www.hootsuite.com) is the best way to manage all your social media accounts efficiently.**

There are so many social media tools now: Facebook, LinkedIn, Twitter, Snapchat, Instagram, Google+, Pinterest, Myspace, etc. So what's the best way to manage all your social media accounts?

Hootsuite.

Download it. It's a social media management dashboard where users can manage all their accounts through a centralized platform.

Instead of manually posting on every one of your social media accounts individually, connect your accounts to Hootsuite and send messages out to all your networks with one post and mouse click.

4 Ways To Increase Your Social Media Followers

As a business or brand, you should use social media only if people care about you. They can care about you for many reasons, such as:

- Good content you put out

- Great products or services you offer

There's really no point in using social media if nobody knows about you.

Here are some ways to grow your following:

1) **Use your existing followings on social media to cross promote each other.**

For example, if you have 1,000 people Liking your Facebook Fan Page, then encourage them to follow you on Twitter or Instagram. You can add some urgency by giving away freebies to the first 1,000 followers... say something like, "I'll send all new followers a private link that gives them access to a special coupon or product [of course, you must fulfill this]."

2) Find similar social media in your niche and swap promotions with them.

If you have 5,000 Twitter followers in the investment space, then find another Twitter user in the investment space who also has 5,000 followers and ask him if you can cross-promote each other. This is a quick and easy way to build up followers.

It sounds like it could be a lot of work, but any marketer or entrepreneur should know other people in their industry well. There shouldn't be much research or "icebreaking" required.

3) Pay folks with big followings to recommend you.

Find experts in your niche who have audiences that can help you. Contact these experts and propose paying them for any traffic they send your way. You can start by paying them $1 per follower or Like you receive. Bigger names will want a lot more… as much as $7 per person.

I've run several successful campaigns utilizing this strategy. The leads were better than I thought, and I "paid for performance," which is the best way to pay for advertising, since everyone wins.

4) **Use hashtags.**

Hashtags are key words preceded with a pound sign: #hello. Social media users insert hashtags for fun. Seriously. There's no other reason.

But thanks to that, marketers can generate a lot of momentum from nothing by utilizing hashtags. When people click on a #hashtag that they see somewhere else, the door is left open for them to find your post. So if you post something good (like a picture, video, or article), then more people will follow you.

Instagram gives results on how many posts there are with any individual hashtag.

If you need help with any of these social media strategies, feel free to e-mail me at naresh dot vissa at gmail dot com.

Best Days And Times To Post On Social Media

Social media is becoming a part of the corporate world. Staffing agency Intelligent Office found that 30% of all employees spend at least an hour a day on social media while at work. Professor Joe Nandhakumar at Warwick Business School also found that social media use increases creativity, collaboration and productivity.

So what does this mean?

People are using social media at work – whether for professional or personal purposes. They use it when they're bored.

There are all sorts of combinations that researchers have published on optimal times to post on social media. Over the years, I've tested them. This is what days and times have worked best for me:

- Facebook – Wednesday around 3:00pm ET

- Instagram – Thursday around 3:00pm ET (Throwback Thursday #tbt)

- Twitter – Go to www.Tweriod.com to see when your Twitter followers are most active.

- LinkedIn – Monday-Thursday around 8:00am or 5:30pm ET

- Google+ – Monday-Thursday around 10am ET

- Pinterest – Friday after 8pm ET or Saturday anytime until 4pm ET

Social marketing publisher Social Caffeine published research on social media posting times, and it lined up very similarly to my own experiences. I'm not going to delve into why these days and times make sense. There could be a multitude of reasons and theories.

Like e-mails, social media that are time sensitive – like Twitter and LinkedIn – are most effective within a few hours after they're sent. The longer time passes, the less traction they'll have.

Facebook posts, on the other hand, can gain more visibility and face time as they age over a short window (within 30 hours). This is because of Facebook's News Feed algorithm – it highlights posts that are relevant or popular regardless of how old they are.

Generally speaking, weekdays during work hours are great times to post text-oriented messages. Creative posts – like pictures on Pinterest or Instagram – tend to garner more attention on Saturdays.

Social Media Resource

Hootsuite (www.hootsuite.com) is the best way to manage all your social media accounts efficiently.

Chapter 8:
HOW TO CREATE BENEFICIAL FACEBOOK MARKETING CAMPAIGNS

Social media marketing is improving by the month, and Facebook is leading the pack. Facebook has nearly 2 billion users (as of October 2015). That's a bunch of people to market to. As a result, Facebook has put many resources into improving its ease of use for marketers so they can easily target an audience.

Users on Facebook share their information not just with their friends but also with Facebook. Facebook knows a user's age, sex, location (permanent and temporary), education, work history, hobbies, interests, friends, and more.

As an advertiser, you can use all this information to your benefit when running targeted ad campaigns.

For example, an owner of a dance club asked me how to find people in the area who liked a certain band from the 80's because the band was going to be performing at his club.

That's such a niche market to advertise to, but thanks to Facebook, he could find exactly who satisfied these criteria. There is no other platform that would allow you to run a search for these key terms and spit back worthwhile results.

We targeted an ad campaign on Facebook to approximately 20 people within a 50-mile radius of the venue. Facebook made sure these people saw the ads for this event. Tickets to the concert ended up selling out, and most of the attendees said they found out about the event through Facebook (ads and the Fan Page).

For physical service businesses (dentists, restaurants, gyms, etc.), offers work very well. These "flash deals" can be timely discounts or giveaways. In other words, you can create your own Groupon type of deal through Facebook. You can offer coupons, free appetizers, teeth whitening, one-week free gym memberships, etc. and target people in your area. Offers have the best chance of going viral because Facebook will automatically have your customers share them with their networks. So make sure your offer is AMAZING. Discount at least 50%, and publicize it. Show the original price (crossed out) and the discounted price.

Additionally, consider advertising to the fan pages of people who have thousands of "Likes" in your niche or industry. Propose paying them for traffic they send your way. You can start by paying them $1 per follower or Like you receive. If they forward their followers to an external squeeze page to collect name or product promotion, then you can work out a deal and track all that data. I recommend you use Mixpanel (www.mixpanel.com) to create and track uniquely coded links.

Facebook advertising is pay per click – meaning, you only pay when someone clicks your ad. Advertising within the U.S. costs as low as $0.05 per click, and advertising to Facebook users outside the US is incredibly cheap – as low as $0.02 a click. That's a steal compared to what you'd pay for an effective Google AdWords or Yahoo Gemini campaign (at least $0.15 per click).

Facebook is also great for mobile. Nielsen reported that mobile APPLICATIONS (apps) now account for 90% of all time users spend on their smartphones and tablets, and Consumer Intelligence Research Partners (CIRP) found Facebook to be the most used app. This presents a tremendous advertising opportunity within Facebook.

Facebook advertising can accomplish six different purposes:

1) Increase your Likes

2) Market your posts to increase engagement – comments, shares and overall virality

3) Send traffic to your external site

4) Convert users into Likes or quality leads

5) Convert users into customers

6) Reach a target market

14 Steps To Set Up Facebook Ads

Facebook has done a great job of making user advertising incredibly self-explanatory and simple. For the newbies, you can follow these simple steps:

1) **Use Google Chrome.** Facebook's Power Editor program creates ads best, and Chrome is most compatible with it.

2) **Log into your Facebook account.**

3) **On the left sidebar, click "Create Ad."**

4) **Follow the steps to create your advertisement.**

5) **Play around with all the Power Editor features.**

6) **Right-rail ads convert best.** Facebook announced that it optimized its right hand column ads, and the results have been noteworthy. Advertisers are seeing higher conversion rates, and users are noticing and reading them.

7) **As you follow the steps, upload a creative image and ONE SENTENCE of copy text with a clear call to action.**

8) **Be sure to enter your address if you're a physical business.** This will help target people in your proximity.

9) **Facebook doesn't allow you to target multiple cities in multiple countries.** You'll have to stick to one country and multiple cities within that country. To hit more countries, you can create a duplicate ad and select a different country.

10) **You can pick where you want your ads to display, i.e. left sidebar, News Feed, mobile (iOS or Android), tablet, desktop, etc.**

11) **Facebook even allows you to advertise to your competitors' customers.**

12) **If you have a mailing list, then create a "Similar/Lookalike Audience."** This will allow you to upload your existing mailing list to Facebook, and then Facebook will analyze the people on your list who are on Facebook and come up with more targets who are similar to those on your list. This is a great example of e-mail marketing transforming into social media marketing effectively.

13) **Your e-mail list is much more proven than any social media.** You will receive greater ROI through your e-mail list than advertising to leads from your e-mail list on Facebook. If you have the option of marketing to your e-mail list or Facebook, always pick your e-mail list.

14) **Run multiple campaigns so you can test to see what works best.**

How To Advertise Free On Facebook

If you don't want to dabble with Facebook's paid advertising platform, that's OK. There are ways you can get your word out without spending money.

My favorite way is to join Facebook groups that relate directly to my product. For example, last year, I released a book on podcasting (actually, it's *The* Book Of Podcasting). I joined as many Facebook groups relating to podcasting as I could. I contacted the admins of the groups and sent them free copies of my book. Most of them liked it and recommended it to their groups. That helped my sales tremendously during the book's launch.

3 Ways To Optimize The Facebook News Feed

1) **Post engaging content.**

Facebook ranks and publishes on News Feed based on ENGAGEMENT, which consists mostly of Likes and comments. So when you post something on Facebook, make sure it's worthwhile. Posts that aren't engaging dilute your brand and "post value", which means future posts won't get the visibility they deserve.

2) **Even if you post a link or anecdote, include a question for people to answer.**

Questions in status updates and posts get more replies (increasing engagement) than a bunch of declarative sentences. This is because questions are call to actions. They add urgency to people reacting.

3) **Respond to comments, particularly during the first couple of hours.**

A Facebook post's peak visibility comes immediately after it's posted. If engagement is low 2-3 hours after posting, then News Feed will stop promoting it for free.

This means Facebook posters should reply to comments sooner rather than later. Do not post something and then check it the next day... chances are, you will have "missed out" on a free "gimme opportunity."

I even know one guy who tags and thanks every person who Likes his post in the comments section. He may not realize it, but what he's doing is artificially boosting his post's engagement, thus setting off signals within Facebook's algorithms to boost the post higher on people's News Feeds.

If Facebook or social media intimidates you, but you'd still like to test some things out, don't hesitate to reach out to me at naresh dot Vissa at Gmail dot com and I can help walk you through the process.

Chapter 9:
HOW TO BE DISCOVERED ON LINKEDIN

D o you want clients, customers, affiliates, or employers to find you? Get on LinkedIn, and make your profile public. That's how I landed the perfect job.

Since the summer after my first year of college, I provided booking services to radio shows across the country. I started out as an intern of the now-defunct BizRadio Network and then branched out and added several other radio shows to my repertoire. Guests on my shows included Congressman Ron Paul, Al Jazeera's Ali Velshi (CNN at the time), Girls Gone Wild founder Joe Francis, and authors Michael Lewis and Robert Kiyosaki. By the end of my senior year of college, I had three years of production and hosting experience for nearly ten business shows while booking more than 700 experts in the fields of finance, economics, business management, entrepreneurship, self-help, leadership, sales and marketing.

Despite my work, I couldn't find a decent full-time gig in media. I spoke with contacts at Bloomberg, CNBC and FOX, and they all said I needed more experience. Despite their rejections, I didn't lose faith in my abilities. But once I started graduate school at Duke, I finally threw in the towel.

Enter LinkedIn

I use most major social media networks, and I generally keep my settings private. However, I have always made LinkedIn public.

People use LinkedIn to network *professionally*: find jobs, seek clients, and explore talent. The site solves a bunch of recruitment pains, so why would professionals want to hide themselves and their strengths?

A director at the largest private investment publisher in the world used LinkedIn to find me while I was finishing school. In his introductory message, he stated, "We aren't acquainted, but I found your profile on LinkedIn and wanted to reach out to say hello… I want to see if you had some time to get on a call to discuss an opportunity we have in the works that may be of interest to you."

The firm wanted me to help start an entirely new division: an online radio station. I'm sure there were many other qualified candidates from the national networks I mentioned, but because I used LinkedIn effectively, I seemed to be a perfect candidate in the eyes of the company's hiring managers. During my time at the firm, our radio network turned a corner to grow into a profitable, expandable, seven-figure enterprise.

I'm not saying professionals should depend solely on LinkedIn to find business. I might be considered a rare occurrence of LinkedIn success. Nevertheless, if you're confident about your experience and abilities, why would you keep your profile private? Had I done that, chances are… my talents would be rotting away elsewhere, and this book wouldn't be in front of you today.

4 Ways To Market On LinkedIn

LinkedIn is the leading social network for professionals. I started using it when I was a student, and it helped me target companies and individuals during my internship and job searches. It also allowed recruiters to find me, which is how I landed my first ever full-time job out of graduate school.

Here are some ways to use LinkedIn for your company or brand:

1) **Create individual and company profiles.**

   In your company profile, fill everything out. Update it frequently with your latest products, deals and offerings.

2) **Join target groups and engage in discussion in them.**

Groups allow you access to other individuals and companies. The more you put you and your company out there, the more people will recognize and come to respect you and your work.

3) Advertise

LinkedIn has a lot of professional information on its users. You can advertise through LinkedIn's advertising interface by visiting the "Business Services" tab at the top of your LinkedIn page and clicking "Advertise."

Advertising campaigns are very similar to Facebook and pay per click ads. You can set your own budget and decide whom you'd like to target.

4) Post

If you *really* want to build a loyal and true following while establishing credence on a grand scale, then post about topics you have knowledge in.

LinkedIn's Influencer program curates posts from 500 of the world's top thought leaders. Becoming an Influencer requires a lot of solid writing, but that's why LinkedIn released its Pulse platform – a social professional news publication that curates the best posts on LinkedIn.

Pulse is quickly becoming a go-to source for professional content, so if you write well on topics that interest the public, then LinkedIn will feature your post.

As of September 2015, LinkedIn has more than 400 million users. These people all have access to Pulse. **No other advertising channel or publication can compete with LinkedIn's publishing clout now.**

To post on Pulse, go to your page's "Posts" section, select "Write a new post," share your expertise and knowledge, and then hit the publish button. If it's good enough, you'll be marketed prominently, and the piece will make its rounds across your niche.

People will start following your posts and request to be friends with you. You'll build your brand, name, credibility... pretty much everything for you, your products, services, and your business.

Chapter 10:
3 WAYS TO MARKET ON MESSAGE BOARDS

Standard social media doesn't usually include message boards, but message boards are becoming go-to sources for media and news consummation and are extremely social, since they consist of people interacting with each other on a public and virtual level.

Online message boards have greatly evolved since the advent of the Internet. What AOL and Yahoo once dominated has grown into a noisy yet niche goodwill advertising market.

Now, there are message boards available on any topic: your favorite sports teams, weight loss, divorce, drug addiction, BDSM, suicide execution, necrophilia… pretty much anything. Even better, every niche has one or two gargantuan message boards with thousands of users. Those are the message boards you want to leverage to market your product or service.

So if you're a divorce lawyer, join the Lawyers.com Community or Men's Divorce Forum and start posting threads and answering posters' questions. You'll build up your respectability, credibility, and brand, and concurrently, people in that community will come to you when they need divorce services.

Three message boards in particular carry so many topics, niches and discussion and have great search engine optimization (SEO) value:

1) Yahoo Answers

   If you Google any question or problem, there's a good chance the first listing that comes up will be something from Yahoo Answers. While the quality of the questions, answers and discussion may seem comical, the search engine optimization (SEO) value of the site still makes joining this community and engaging with it worthwhile. It's a great place to provide quality answers while also plugging your business, product or website.

2) Reddit

   The Reddit user base is almost cultish. People, reporters, scam artists, companies, and brands can hide behind their usernames. As a result, Reddit has reported breaking news and other crazy stories.

   Additionally, Reddit has raised millions of dollars for charity. For example, in 2010, users raised more than $185,000 for relief efforts after the earthquake in Haiti. In 2014, more than 200,000 users in nearly 190 countries broke the Guinness World Record for the largest Secret Santa gift exchange ever. Almost $700,000 was spent on gift purchases and shipping costs. The money that Reddit's users have been able to cough up shows the power of the discussion board.

Reddit AMAs ("Ask Me Anything") are platforms for unique individuals to answer questions about anything. Celebrities give AMAs every day, but even little guys like me can have what are called IAmA (I am a...). When I released my book PODCASTNOMICS, I hosted an IAmA (IAmA Author of PODCASTNOMICS and have Generated Millions Of Dollars Through Podcasting. AMA!), and the focus was on podcasting. Complete strangers asked me anything from how to start a podcast to how to make money off podcasts. The AMA ended up generating book sales for me, and it's still on the Reddit forum archives, so anyone can find it years after it took place.

To do an IAmA or a version of an AMA, sign up for a free username to Reddit and then Google, "Reddit IAmA." Click the first site that pops up, and then you'll find instructions on the right sidebar of Reddit to get started.

3) Quora

Quora is a professional site. It's not as shady as Reddit, and not as comedic as Yahoo Answers. It requires users to use their real names to log in. Many users sign in to Quora through their Google, Facebook or Twitter profiles… meaning it's much more difficult for people to hide.

The media pays particular interest to the topics discussed on Quora. If they like what they see, there's a good chance they'll reprint your content or contact you to be a source as an expert.

Chapter 11:
HOW ONLINE LISTINGS AND REVIEWS CAN AFFECT YOUR BUSINESS

*T*his *chapter is a little different. It's centered around an anecdote, which should teach you about the importance of getting your business listed on "online yellow pages" like Yelp, TripAdvisor, and Google Local Listings. It can also tell you about the powerful effect of public online reviews on any business.*

One Sunday afternoon, I was looking for a place that was still open for lunch around 2:30. I pulled out my Yelp app and found a decently rated Indian restaurant close-by. It's was above three stars but below four – mediocre, but not amazing or terrible.

I drove to the restaurant and ate their lunch buffet. The food was like its reviews: average at best. I paid my bill with tip for $17.

A few days later, I noticed an extra charge (on top of the $17 one) from the restaurant on my credit card. It was for nearly $18. I thought they likely double-billed me by swiping my card twice and adding a dollar to the second swipe, or they put someone else's meal on my card (meaning the other person signed with an unauthorized signature).

I called the restaurant to let them know about this. The manager apologized and told me I could drop by the restaurant to eat a free buffet lunch. I told her that the buffet wouldn't be free since I was already charged $18 extra. I asked for a full refund. She said they don't give refunds because of the long process involved – calling credit card companies, producing receipts, etc. So I asked for two buffets – one of which would be free for me due to their mistake and the inconvenience they were causing.

The manager didn't understand. She couldn't do the math in her head. She had no understanding of customer lifetime value or opportunity cost.

She insisted she could only give me one buffet because she'd be losing money if she gave me two. I told her she wouldn't be losing money on a buffet because she was going to throw out all the leftover food from the buffet when it closed at 3:00 in the afternoon anyway. Unlike *a la carte* orders, buffet food isn't divisible, and there is no extra preparation involved to feed customers.

She said they didn't throw food out but instead gave it to poor people. I didn't feel like debating the merits of that.

I stressed that she took my $18 and was trying to get me to drive 20 minutes to eat crappy food that I never had any intention to pay for in the first place.

Her compromise was that I could eat two weekday buffets, which cost $11 each. My $18 credit would cover the first buffet, and after the second buffet, I'd have to give her $4 in cash... so I'd still be paying $22 for two buffets that cost $22 in total.

"That makes no sense," I said. "You'd still be making me pay for two buffets. I'm the victim here. You screwed me. I don't want your crappy food. Just give me my $18 back, which you stole."

She yelled at me on the phone.

"Sir, I'll be losing money if I give you a free buffet!"

I told her she had no business sense.

Two Indian businesspeople fighting over money on the phone is a pay-per-view event (I'm allowed to say that... because I'm Indian ;-).

She put me on hold for five minutes to look at the receipts. She came back and told me that it appeared someone else's meal was placed on my credit card and that other person never paid. I had no clue if she was telling the truth or not. As a result, she wouldn't even give me one meal – the one I had essentially paid for with the $18 charge. She said they'd go back through their cameras, find whose meal it was, and then contact that person and ask them to pay me directly. Then, I could get my money back. No comp for food or anything... just the hope of getting money from this imaginary person she invented.

That was one of the dumbest things I'd ever heard from a merchant. Who does that?

Before I hung up on her (or maybe she hung up on me?), I issued a threat.

"I'm calling my credit card company to dispute this charge. You'll lose the $18. Then I'll give you terrible reviews on Yelp and Google. And I'll never come back again!"

"Feel free," she said. "It won't matter to us."

So I did it...

The credit card company disputed the transaction and credited the $18 charge to my account.

I wrote one-star reviews on Yelp and Google Local Listings. I laid out the facts in a few sentences without libeling the restaurant. I even named the manager in my reviews for proof that I wasn't making shit up. Here's the gist of what I said:

They double-billed my credit card. When I called to settle the transaction, they said they accidentally put someone else's meal on my card. They said they needed to get in touch with the other person who didn't pay, so they asked for my number and said they'd get back with me. Who does that? They refused to refund (even though I had my transaction history and receipt proving I was duped). They wouldn't even comp me with food.

As for the food, it is no good for vegetarians. They have all of two veg options for the buffet.

An hour later, the manager called me back. She said they were going to refund the $18 and that I could come in for a free lunch buffet, but that it would have to be "today between 2:00 and 2:30."

Fortunately, I had no pressing work or meetings that afternoon. I drove to the restaurant... walked in... and before grabbing a plate, the manager said, "Sir, we can only give you this meal if you remove any negative reviews you may have posted online."

Seriously? AHA!

I told her I'd remove the reviews when I got home since smartphone apps couldn't remove them.

I ate the meal, drove him, and stayed true to my word and removed the reviews.

2 Ways To Leverage Online Listings And Reviews To Affect Your Business

The story I just told lays out two key takeaways:

1) **Get your business listed on:**

   Yelp –
   https://biz.yelp.com/signup_business/new

   TripAdvisor –
   www.tripadvisor.com/GetListedNew

   Google   Local   Listings –
   www.google.com/mybusiness

   Yellow   Pages –
   https://adsolutions.yp.com/listings/basic

   Yahoo   Local –
   https://smallbusiness.yahoo.com/local-listings?s_local=add

   SureCritic - email sales@surecritic.com with your business info

These directories are now the most popular and search-friendly online yellow pages. Your business has a chance to be found, and all of them have options to list your business completely free of charge. I would've never discovered this Indian restaurant if I was aimlessly driving around. I had to take out my Yelp app to find them.

While the aforementioned list of directories is a must-do for all businesses, don't forget to be on popular directories within your niche. For example, if you're a lawyer, you'll want to be on www.avvo.com. Or if you're a doctor, having good reviews on the following sites will help your practice tremendously:

RateMDs – www.ratemds.com

Healthgrades – www.healthgrades.com

ZocDoc – www.zocdoc.com

Vitals – www.vitals.com

To find your profession's rating/review sites, Google [your profession] + "ratings reviews"].

As we've established in this book, people make decisions – such as where they're going to eat or what hotel to stay at – based on information they can find online. Gone are the days of "checking places out."

Don't be afraid of getting negative reviews. Your business has a lot more to gain by being on these listings than to lose by not being on them. Your goal is to be found first. The positive reviews can come second.

If you have negative reviews or negative content about you on the Internet and want them removed, then contact me at naresh dot vissa at gmail dot com and I should be able to find solutions for you. You can search SEO reputation experts on Fiverr or Upwork, but finding good ones who won't screw up your other search listings may be a challenge.

2) **Encourage your customers to write good reviews.**

If you're a restaurant/bar/club, give them a free drink or appetizer if they take out their phones and write a review while they're in your place. Make them show you the review to get the freebie.

If you're a business, give away something of value (free consultation, free toothpaste/toothbrush/mouthwash if you're a dentist, free one-month subscription, etc.) in exchange for a review on one of the directories.

People care about reviews. They decide which doctor or lawyer to go to or where to eat based on online reviews.

So as a business owner or marketer, you should care about your reviews too – for better or for worse.

In my case, this restaurant didn't take me seriously until I wrote negative reviews. Once they saw them, they did anything to appease me to get me to remove those reviews... and I did. That, to them, was worth more than the $18... because the Internet leaves a permanent mark on one's history and reputation, which can, in turn, determine success or failure.

3) Resource: www.productsforreview.com

Products For Review allows marketers to get reviews of their products. For $10, submit a product for review and the site will send your query out to a broad list of potential reviewers, who will contact you for a sample if they're interested.

Chapter 12:
3 WAYS TO IMPROVE WEB SEARCH ENGINE OPTIMIZATION (SEO)

Search engine optimization (SEO) is the process of affecting a site's presence on a search engine (Google). In other words, good SEO means when someone Googles you, favorable search results show up on the first page. Bad SEO means that bad or irrelevant search results show up.

So if someone Googles "Michael Jordan" with the intent of learning more about the up-and-coming actor from FRUITVALE STATION or *Friday Night Lights* and they only find results and information on the famous basketball player, then that would be considered bad SEO for the actor Michael B. Jordan but great SEO for the athlete Michael Jordan.

As a marketer or entrepreneur, you want to ensure that you are found when people search for relevant key words to your name, business, industry, and market. The strategies laid out in previous chapters and throughout this book (blogging, content marketing, podcasting, YouTube, etc.) optimize search results in your favor.

You'll want to consider these simple ideas to play your SEO scorecard safe:

1) **Build your site on WordPress.**

WordPress now powers more than 100 million websites and is the most used web content management system (CMS) in the world because its portal makes it simple for anyone to set up and update a site. On top of that, it's free!

WordPress designs and automated functions come with clean code. Consequently, WordPress sites are extremely Google search friendly.

You can get started on creating your website yourself by visiting www.WordPress.com. If you don't want to spend a day or two of time on doing it yourself, then it would be most efficient to go to www.upwork.com (formerly Elance/oDesk) and hire someone with five stars to create a fully functioning WordPress site with all your specs for less than $150 (assuming a simple site).

2) **Include tags and descriptions when you create pages and posts.**

WordPress gives users options to fill out keywords and tags for every page they create. Because this is an option, many non-technical web managers neglect to fill this out.

That's why this gets its own section: it's that important to fill out every page's tags, keywords, description, excerpt, category, and every other option given in the WordPress posting/publishing portal. The more words and key words you put in, the better.

3) **Go to Fiverr or Upwork (formerly Elance/oDesk) to hire someone with five stars to do SEO on your site for less than $50.**

There is an entire industry built around the WordPress platform, so there are plentiful experts to help you with design, development and SEO.

SEO experts through third-party vendors like Fiverr will skyrocket your website rankings on Google by optimizing the best keywords through link building.

Don't worry if you don't understand the previous paragraph because the person you hire will do this for such a low cost. SEO is a science for experienced, technical webmasters, so it'll be well worth your time paying someone less than $50 to get you and your site up to speed rather than learning this on your own.

If you have any questions about SEO or hiring third-party contractors, feel free to e-mail me at Naresh dot Vissa at Gmail dot com.

And to receive additional tips on online marketing hacks, you can subscribe FREE to my e-mail list / newsletter at www.nareshvissa.com.

Chapter 13:
3 WAYS TO MAKE MONEY OFF CRAIGSLIST

Craigslist is the most popular digital classified ad platform. It offers thousands of marketplaces based on city or region. Per Alexa rankings, it's one of the top ten most visited sites in the U.S. with more than ten million visits a day.

I've used Craigslist to sell my belongings and other products. I've also used it to buy furniture and electronics, find apartment rentals, and plan bachelor parties.

Some industries that perform best on Craigslist: education, business consulting (accounting, legal, HR/recruitment, etc.), automotive, entertainment (adult and kids), handiwork, fitness, real estate, furniture, and electronics. If you provide a service or function in the service industry, then you need to post on Craigslist.

Like many of the other directories and forums, Craigslist is free and self-explanatory to use. So there's no excuse for a business not to test it out.

Here are the three most important elements of a Craigslist ad:

1) Catchy title

In the old days of classified ads and the Yellow Pages, the best headline got the most eyeballs and attention. That same practice holds true on Craigslist.

2) At least one picture

Craigslist has developed a brand of being shady. It's an online classifieds section after all. Thefts and deaths are more common through Craigslist than most other online marketplaces. Law Street Media found that nearly 90 deaths have been linked to Craigslist.

This is scary, but it's still a popular and efficient site. You can mitigate your own shadiness by posting at least one picture of you, your product, service, company logo, or anything else that's relevant. This will be of huge value to people who find you.

A generic Craigslist ad like, "Asian Massage – come to xyz address for massage," with no pictures, website, or phone number will scare people away (most likely from the POPO).

3) Website

Pictures make you seem less shady. A website makes you seem legit. If you can forward your readers to a professional site or URL outside of Craigslist, then you're ahead of 99% of the competition. Put your website link in the body of your advertising copy.

Craigslist can come across as sketchy. The good news is: you don't have to give away any of your personal info like your email or cell number in your ad. The Craigslist marketplace is set up so that buyers and sellers can contact each other through Craigslist.

Note: the second-most popular digital classifieds site is Backpage.com, though it's turned into a go-to for "back page" type of services. If you're a business that offers one of those services, then this book could be beneficial to you too.

Chapter 14:
HOW ADVERTISING ON PORN SITES CAN GROW YOUR BUSINESS COST-EFFECTIVELY

Porn sites are worth testing ads on. Not many companies do it because of the stigma attached to sex and pornography. As a result, ad rates on porn sites are low – about 1/10 the cost of advertising on mainstream channels like Google AdWords or Facebook.

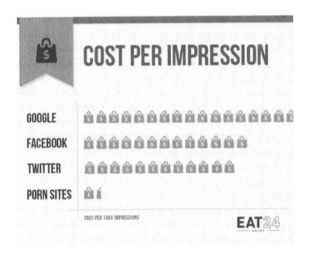

Porn sites have some of the most engaging users on the web. People visit them with an intention, forming an entirely new and untapped market in the process.

Bounce rates are low. Session lengths are high (nearly 20 minutes).

ExtremeTech found that 30% of all Internet traffic goes to pornography or other sexual material. To put that number into context, the Huffington Post reported that more people visit porn sites than they do Netflix, Amazon, and Twitter combined. Xvideos, the largest porn site on the net, has more than five billion visits a month – three times the size of CNN or ESPN.

Now do you see the opportunity?

Consider the case of food delivery company EAT24. They gave porn marketing a shot. Here's what they found:

- **Banners on individual video pages performed five times (5X) better than banners on the homepage** (suggesting that the homepage of a porn site means, "let's not waste time and get down to business").

- **Porn ads carried three times more impressions than Google, Twitter and Facebook ads combined**. Put simply, if you advertise on porn sites, you'll get a ton of visibility... because nobody else is advertising on them (unlike Google, Twitter and Facebook, where most businesses first go to for advertising).

- **New customer retention from porn sites was four times (4x) greater than new customer retention from Facebook**. So the quality of the traffic and leads from porn is high.

In the end, EAT24's porn campaign reached a new market quickly at a low cost. Their porn ads are still running. And the company is bigger now than it has ever been.

How To Advertise On Porn Sites

If you're now intrigued and want to explore more on porn advertising for yourself, then visit the top three porn sites and contact them (note: I won't be providing links or hyperlinks to these sites, so you'll have to Google them):

- YouPorn

- Xvideos

- PornHub

You can advertise with them directly, or one or two of them may refer you to an ad network that will allow you to advertise on many more sites.

To advertise effectively on porn sites, the messaging has to fit the audience and the general theme of sex.

EAT24 had copy like, "WANT BLT WITH YOUR BDSM?" next to an image of a BLT sandwich.

Let's say you're trying to sell precious metals. You'll want to tie your copy or ad image back to sex. Maybe create an image of a 24-karat gold flogger and have copy that says, "Acquire the powers of the Midas Touch. Click here."

Or if you're selling real estate, have an image of a spacious and luxurious bedroom and say, "Red Rooms Available. Click Here To Buy Yours Today."

Anything can be sexually twisted. That's the only way ads on porn sites can stand a chance of succeeding.

If you end up trying advertising on porn sites, I want to hear from you on how it went. Feel free to let me know by e-mailing Naresh dot Vissa at Gmail dot com.

Chapter 15:
WHY CONTENT SHOULD BE MARKETED... AND WHY YOUR MARKETING SHOULD HAVE CONTENT

Content marketing is the use of content to drive more awareness to a brand or product. The end goal of a content marketing strategy is to get readers to take action. The caveat is that the content *shouldn't* incorporate explicit sales messaging. It should be material that readers look forward to reading... so much to the point that they engage with the content and share it with their social networks. That's why content marketing is a long-term strategy that can take years to generate a return... but it builds up immense readership and loyalty to make conversions easy.

The content can be editorial – such as articles or blog posts – or it can be hidden marketing copy – like sales letters or landing pages. Sales letters and landing pages don't sound like engaging content, but the best marketing copywriters know how to disguise sales letters and messaging as good content. They suck readers into a good story and then get them to take action at the end – whether it's buying a product, subscribing to a free newsletter, or dialing a phone number.

A perfect example of this is the video "End of America." You can view the full video by going on YouTube and searching "Stansberry End of America" to see what I'm talking about. The content stretches over an hour long, but the narrative is so strong that it keeps viewers engaged the entire time... and at the end, you – as the viewer – are so convinced on what you read/watched that you feel obligated to buy something.

The "End of America" video became one of the most successful sales videos of all time. It was passed around among fiscally conservative networks and generated hundreds of thousands of brand new, paying customers for Porter Stansberry. It changed online video marketing forever.

Execution means everything in business, and marketing is a part of any execution. But in the digital space, content is still king... not as an editorial play but as a strategic ploy.

Historically, brands have had to "rent" space to get their messages out into the public – through airtime, TV/radio spots, banners, mailing lists, etc. But with content marketing, brands can create their own content to control their marketing messages. They don't have to sit back anxiously to see how their investment in external marketing campaigns performed. They have total autonomy in attracting customers to sell their products or services.

Content marketing – in the form of blogs, vlogs (video blogs), podcasts (audio blogs), e-books, social media, and other channels –attracts *organic* traffic to your content. These are people who *find you* through search, social media, or some other random way. They come pre-qualified.

The more content you generate to build up your brand, the greater you build virtual relationships with your fans, who in turn can become future customers. Good content will establish you as a thought leader or authority figure… someone who can be trusted as a go-to source for advice and information.

The uses of content have enhanced and shifted over millennia. Coming up in this chapter and the next few chapters are some ideas on how you can use content marketing to take your brand and sales to the next level.

Why FREE Reports Are The Best Content Marketing Tools To Grow A Mailing List

The quickest way to grow a mailing list is to give away something of value completely free of charge. Free reports (otherwise called special reports or whitepapers) are a form of content marketing because they provide premium educational information of value that most people would have to pay for. Here are examples of what content businesses can give away free:

- FREE special report

- E-book

- Special audio or video interview

- One-year free trial subscription to an info product

You want to highlight your giveaway as much as possible. The copy should clearly say what you're giving away, why it's of value, and how people can take advantage of this offer (i.e. "Enter Your E-mail Address Below To Get Your FREE XYZ").

Chapter 16:
HOW BLOGGING CAN PRODUCE REVENUE

In the earlier days of the Internet, blogging meant getting a Xanga and posting anything and everything with the hopes that the world would find you. Now, the big blog services are Blogger (blogspot) and microblogs like Tumblr and Twitter. Facebook and LinkedIn also have blogging capabilities through status updates and LinkedIn's Pulse posting platform.

Businesses can blog without getting on specific sites like Blogger or Tumblr. They can host their own blogs through a web domain they own so individuals can find content directly on their sites.

The key to blogging is still the same: come out with new, unique and compelling content to attract readers. Be creative. Incorporate art. Embed audio and video. Inspire, depress, rant, and attack. These readers will end up becoming your biggest advocates – and customers.

9 Ways To Blog Successfully

1) Expert contribution

Big names generate more traction. For example, if you reference Congressman Ron Paul in a blog post about racism, there's a good chance millions of Paul followers and groups will have a Google Alert set on his name – meaning, your blog post will alert them because you mentioned his name in your piece.

This is why so many financial bloggers incorporate ticker symbols into their writing… because so many financial content aggregators are scouring the web for as much relevant information they can find on publicly traded companies.

Getting primary content from influencers is most effective – quoting them, interviewing them, even having them guest post. The *Huffington Post* solicits content from freelance experts, thought leaders, and reporters. It chooses the best submitted content and publishes it on its site. It doesn't pay its contributors, who submit content to build up their brands and visibility.

In 2011, AOL bought the *Huffington Post* for $315 million. The *Huffington Post* model proves that you can get a bunch of other people to do most of the work and you can still create high value for readers.

Paying a big name to blog for you could be a worthwhile investment because that big name will share their work with their networks. Just being associated with this big name will also add credibility to your brand.

2) Curate

Content curation is the process of picking and summarizing the best content that is relevant to a particular audience. It is a great way to pump out content without much ideation or creativity.

The best example of content curation is *Business Insider*, which has hundreds of editors and reporters who summarize hot stories in their own words. To readers, it seems as if they're reading a primary source. In a sense, *Business Insider* passes off these stories as their own to the reader, even though they fully hyperlink and source to the original sources.

Business Insider rarely comes out with anything new or noteworthy. It presents existing topical news and summarizes it for readers.

In September 2015, Business Insider was sold to German publisher Axel Springer at a $442 million valuation.

What does *Business Insider*'s success mean to content creators? It means that you can use other people's content, change the headlines, summarize their pieces, and pump out a ton of these stories to attract and engage audiences.

In the digital era, there is so much information being put out. People don't want to read it all. Instead, they want to get an easy gist of what's most important.

3) Frequent content

Release LOTS of content. It keeps your audience engaged. It also improves your search engine optimization (SEO) tremendously because you're creating a lot of backlinks and using search terms by writing and publishing more.

This sounds daunting, but it's a lot easier than you'd think...

The first step is to do what we've already covered in this section: reprint expert and guest contributions free of charge. Curate other people's stories.

You can visit Guest Post Articles (www.guestpostarticles.com) to post a listing to accept content on your site. Guest Post Articles is a marketplace that helps match guest bloggers, article writers, and marketers with blogs and website publishers who want guest posts, articles, and reviews to post online.

Then, to take things to the next level, find college upperclassmen who are double majors in journalism or English and whatever area your content covers. Graduate students will be interested too.

Hire as many students you want as freelance writing contractors, and pay them $10 per article they write. Their names don't have to be on all the posts. They can be ghostwriters. You can easily come out with a piece every day... and since you run the show, you can put your name on all the pieces.

So many outlets already do this. How do I know this? Because I ghostwrite for some big corporations.

Finding writers isn't as hard as it seems either. I know because I used to be one of those writers who begged for a $10 per article gig back when I was a student. It's great experience for youngsters looking to break into the publishing industry and beef up their resumes.

4) Timely or controversial topics

Write about the hot topics… because everyone's talking about them!

And remember… controversy will produce lovers and haters… but it gets people talking!

It's even OK to talk shit in your posts. Criticize other big companies or individuals, but also provide ideas for improvement. This is a great way for your words to go viral, but it also opens you up to criticism… and lots of opportunity to sell yourself or your product.

5) List

In general, numbers in headlines are good – i.e. "4 Ways To Improve Your Life", "10 Hacks To Get Free Airline Tickets", etc. These posts get straight to the point and give readers exactly what they're seeking.

6) Explain how or why

"How To" is a great way to start a headline – i.e. "How To Get A Girlfriend", "How To Eat A Triple Pound Hotdog", etc. The same applies to "Why" – "Why Guys Like To Drink", "Why India And Pakistan Can't Be Friends", etc. Walk readers through the entire process – step-by-step. This will provide tremendous value to folks, thus resulting in great SEO and a plethora of other opportunities, including readers or fans for life.

7) Enable and respond to comments

With the Internet, creating a community around content is now easier than ever. As a content marketer, your goal is to form a tight-knit, long-lasting community of readers who will market for you – for better (as a lover) or worse (as a critic).

Comments allow people to voice their opinions on your work. Many times, comments are more entertaining or actionable than the post itself.

As the content creator, you should moderate all comments and respond to them to add a human touch and show your transparency.

8) Post your content on popular platforms or niche publishers

In addition to housing all your content on your website and posting on all social media, you want to disseminate it on other popular platforms as guest posts.

For print (including visuals, pictures, memes, and infographics), syndication through platforms like LinkedIn, *TechCrunch* and

Huffington Post is becoming more important to content marketing strategy. Submission to the *Huffington Post* can be selective, but LinkedIn has opened up its publishing platform to all its users. LinkedIn released its Pulse platform – a social professional news publication that curates the best posts on LinkedIn. As of September 2015, LinkedIn has more than 400 million users. With its new Pulse application, LinkedIn gives all its users access to the best curated content according to a user's interests.

Translation: if you write well on topics that interest the public, then LinkedIn will feature your post to your target audience.

Posting content on LinkedIn is quick and easy. All you have to do is copy your blog post from your site on to your LinkedIn page's "Posts" section, select "Write a new post," and paste the post into the content box. Hit the publish button, and if your post is good enough, you'll be marketed prominently, and the piece will make its rounds across your niche.

People will start following your posts and request to be friends with you. You'll build your brand, name, credibility… pretty much everything for you, your products, services, and your business.

I've laid out LinkedIn as one example of a publishing platform for bloggers. There are many others, including *Medium*, *Huffington Post*, Reddit, Tumblr, Quora, Google+, and Facebook fan pages and status updates. You can apply the principles from LinkedIn to all these platforms and really get your content out there.

You should also contact publishers in your niche or industry and ask them if they need additional high quality content. Convince them to republish your work. There are so many publishers and blogs (big and small) in every industry that are dying for great content to feed their readers.

You can visit Guest Post Articles (www.guestpostarticles.com) to submit your content to existing publishers. They will contact you directly if they're interested in reprinting your piece. Guest Post Articles is a marketplace that helps match guest bloggers, article writers, and marketers with blogs and website publishers who want guest posts, articles, and reviews.

Make sure you link back to your website at the end of the post. You can include a disclaimer saying something like, *"This post* *originally appeared on xyz blog. You can read the original post here."* This maximizes all your views.

Contributing to sites like these establishes you as an authority and constructs your brand. The more places you're on, the more leverage you build. These sites also have great SEO, so they'll pop up on the first or second page when you're Googled.

Here are the best platforms to post different kinds of content:

Podcasts – iTunes, TuneIn (www.tunein.com), Stitcher (www.stitcher.com), SoundCloud (www.soundcloud.com), Player FM (www.player.fm), Spreaker (www.spreaker.com) and many other smaller distributors (you can get a full list by purchasing my previous book PODCASTNOMICS: The Book Of Podcasting… To Make You Millions on Amazon)

eBooks – Amazon (Kindle [KDP], paperback [CreateSpace], audiobook [Audible]), Smashwords (www.smashwords.com)

Slide decks – SlideShare (www.slideshare.com)

Videos – YouTube

Webinars – YouTube

9) Incorporate social sharing links before and after your posts

Social sharing links are the little sharing icons you frequently see above or below articles your read. Having them on your site encourages readers to share your content with their networks, which will lead to more hits to your site.

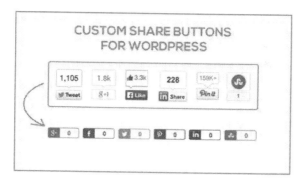

You should include social sharing links above and below your article. This is because readers who make it to the bottom likely won't remember the sharing buttons on the top. You need to put the buttons in their face so they are fully aware what they read can be shared.

Including the social sharing links on your website or posts is rather straightforward. Google "social share buttons plugin on

WordPress", and click the first site that comes up. Download the latest plugin version to your site. You'll then be able to enable the social sharing links through the "Plugins" section in the back-end of your WordPress admin login.

How Blogging Can Grow Your Mailing List

When you reprint your content elsewhere or write for someone else, the bylines/disclaimers at the end of your posts are so important so people can actually visit your site to find out more about you… and to subscribe to your mailing list! As discussed earlier in the book, the mailing list is the single greatest asset you can build as an online businessperson.

To capture names on your website's blog, make sure you have plenty of newsletter opt-in boxes and maybe even a pop-up asking visitors to subscribe to your free mailing list so they can stay up to date on your latest content.

I've even had clients force users to enter their e-mail address in order to get the full content. Take this example from a podcast client: when visitors click the "Play" button or "Listen" for a podcast, a pop-up comes up immediately asking the user to enter their e-mail into a box so they can listen to the episode they clicked on. This seems forceful, but it's a great way to collect new e-mail leads.

How To Connect Your Blog Posts To Your Mailing List

Whatever new content you post on your site, also send it through your mailing list, and vice-versa. Posting content on your site leaves the door open for something to go viral. It improves SEO.

Sending a message to your mailing list directly reaches your subscribers. They don't need to go searching on your website for your information. Mailings are instant and time-sensitive notices that show up in people's mailboxes. The mailing list makes it easier for your readers to consume your content.

In your e-mail templates, make sure you include a link to the original content piece from your website. That way, if someone forwards your e-mail to a friend, the friend can click that link and join your mailing list. Or he/she can share the link with friends, thus driving more traffic to your site and increasing the chances of growing your list.

In the displayed picture, you'll notice the circled text says, "Read this article on the *Moneyball Economics* website by clicking here."

Following An Editorial Schedule

Mailing schedules make editorial and list management organized. By having a calendar or schedule of what you're sending to your list and when you're sending it, you'll be able to plan future sends – on the sales and editorial side – productively.

I share my editorial calendars via Google Sheets (Google's version of Microsoft Excel) with my partners and clients. That way, editors will know their deadlines, and partners will know what to expect in the future.

On your marketing/editorial schedule/calendar, you **never want to send more than one editorial mailing per week**. Earlier in the book, I said it's OK to send frequently to your list… but that's if you're sending sales or marketing messages because you're at least getting a return for your send. If you're sending editorial content, it's best to restrict it to one mailing a day at the absolute maximum.

Nonetheless, you can still send one sales e-mail on top of one editorial e-mail on the same day – meaning, you can send a blog post via e-mail in the morning, and a dedicated sales e-mail in the afternoon. But that's it – never send more than two total e-mails to your list on any given day.

How Blogging Improves Search Engine Optimization

Search engine optimization (SEO) is the process of affecting a site's presence on a search engine (Google). In other words, good SEO means when someone Googles you, favorable search results show up on the first page. Bad SEO means that bad or irrelevant search results show up.

If you market your blog posts the way I tell you to, then they will get the visibility they need. As a result, individual posts – and in turn your website – will show up on search engine results. Other blogs and social media users will link to your blog. The more visibility your blog has, the greater the chance of it ranking highly on Google searches.

How To Make Money Off Blogging

Anyone who can grow their readership can get a leading company in its industry to advertise to it. For example, let's say you create a business that publishes content on organic food. To help bring in more traffic to your site, you could write content relating to organic food. You could also curate a bunch of content or find other people to guest write for you. You could then syndicate the content on several health sites, blogs, LinkedIn, and all the other blog publishing platforms I mentioned (*Medium*, *Huffington Post*, Reddit, Tumblr, Quora, Google+, etc.) to help drive traffic to your site.

You can then sell advertising on your site in the form of banners and space ads / text inserts (more on what these are in the upcoming chapter, "WHY NATIVE ADVERTISING TRUMPS EVERYTHING ELSE).

Once you build your list up, you could then partner with Whole Foods or Organic Valley and sell their products. They will pay you lots of money to advertise to your list! Or you could develop your own product or service and sell it to your list.

Building your readership, web traffic and list will make you a trusted source of information, so selling them your (or someone else's) book, product, services becomes easier than "renting" ad space or "cold calling."

Why Advertising Yourself Is Better Than Advertising Others

Sticking to the organic food blog example…

Advertising from large corporations like Whole Foods or Organic Valley will beef up your brand because of your association with such established entities. In fact, I'd contact such big firms and offer to advertise them and their products completely free of charge. The association with them will be worth it… and chances are, they'll pay you to advertise, even if you offer them free advertising.

But if you can't get any big companies to advertise with you freely, then do not go for smaller, organic food companies to advertise on your site. What good would that do for you? You've spent years building up your following, and you're going to forward all that traffic to someone else who nobody knows? Maybe even a competitor?

That's why you should *advertise yourself*… in other words, don't accept advertising money from some small, rinky-dink company. Instead, plug your own products, services, whitepapers, etc. Selling your own stuff will generate longer-lasting returns for you.

Chapter 17:
WHY NATIVE ADVERTISING IS THE BEST CONTENT MARKETING

Native ads blend into the page or content they're in. Examples include space ad text inserts (examples coming up) and sponsored (paid) content that advertisers will write to build brand awareness or get readers to visit their site. They are different from traditional display ads such as banners and pop-ups, which are losing their luster.

Native ads provide smooth advertising experiences, so the return is higher. Sharethrough/IPG Media Lab found that consumers looked at native ads 53% more frequently than display ads. Sharethrough also found that native ads have content that is more appealing, engaging, and visually pleasing than display ads. Consumers generally hold positive attitudes toward them since they are consumed the same way editorial content is consumed.

How To Create Space Ad Text Inserts In Your Print Content

Space ads, or text inserts, are ads blatantly thrown into print content. The idea is to *insert* something that relates to the content and will get a reader's attention.

Consider this example of how to insert and format a space ad into a blog post or newsletter e-mail send:

"Hello my name is Karpal. I own Sutra Bar. Thank you for visiting my website.

I work 80-hour weeks, mostly during the nights.

———————————

WANT A FREE MARGARITA?

Get your Buy 1, Get 1 FREE margarita coupon by clicking here!

Courtesy of Sutra Bar

———————————

I didn't start Sutra Bar with the hopes of making a million dollars. I love watching people drink and act stupid.

Drinking can be a very fun. If it turns into a lucrative venture for me, then great. I can make money while having fun watching other people have fun.

In the example, the section about the free margarita is the space ad.

If you want to see more examples of native advertisements, then subscribe to my FREE e-mail newsletter by visiting www.nareshvissa.com (this sentence is an example of content marketing!).

Chapter 18:
WHY THE BEST COPYWRITING WILL GENERATE THE HIGHEST RETURNS

I'm going to repeat the title of this chapter – one of the most important principles of marketing:

THE BEST COPYWRITING WILL GENERATE THE BEST RETURNS.

Copy is advertising text. It is meant to persuade people to take action. Most times, this "action" involves taking out a credit card to buy something.

Copywriters are people who write this marketing text. They're the ones who come up with catch slogans in advertisements. They're also the ones who concoct order forms, billboard and banner text, radio ads, and pretty much anything you see or hear involving advertising.

Good copywriters have the ability to sell anything through their words. That's why they demand a pretty penny... because most of the good ones collect royalties for their work.

In the online world, the products marketed with the best copy will always sell well. Very rarely do people actually buy products because of its quality (hence, why

147

I wrote this book). Instead, what they read, see, and hear convinces them.

So as a copywriter, it's so important to **touch people's emotions**... so they can read, see and hear the benefits of taking action.

The **best way to strike nerves with your audience is through storytelling**. People don't jump out of their seats at facts. They jump out when told something truly extraordinary. And that only happens when their emotions are hit. This can only happen through storytelling.

This book will hopefully walk you through different ways to communicate stories and create emotions through copywriting, video, audio, social media, and other channels.

Themes And Topics Copywriters Should Follow

Good copy usually follows at least one of these four *themes*:

1) **Inspirational** – Motivate people to act.

2) **Controversial** – Inform people on a unique topic and get them to act to find out more.

3) **Timely** – Relate to the present and delve deeper into a relevant topic by tying in hot current events and pop culture.

4) **Urgent** – Speed up actions by creating suspense or stressing limited time or availability. You can even lower your prices during a special time period to add more urgency.

There are other themes to improve copy, but I have found those four to be most effective.

Once you have your theme, you'll need to find a topic to write about and twist it to fit the purpose and mission of your end goal. Include action verbs to get readers to do something. I've listed some "trigger words" and topics I have found to be particularly effective because they touch people's emotions:

- Health

- Hope

- Without

- Because

- And

- Money

- Conspiracy

- Banned

- Controversial

- Exposed

- Discover

- FREE

- FREE SHIPPING

- Learn More

- Insider

- Urgent

- Before You Forget

- Deadline

- Limited

- Limited Time Only

- You

These words can tie into any product idea. For example, if you're selling printers and want to tie your copy into *health*, you can talk about how your printer works so well that it will save users heartaches, thus improving their health. Or if you want to tie it into *money*, you can talk about how the ink cartridges work efficiently, thus saving users money. Or, you can get *controversial* and *expose* your top competitor so that people will buy your product.

If something is free, then emphasize it by putting it in all caps. FREE!

People love FREE. So find a way to say something is FREE or comes FREE, and make it stand out.

Assume the reader is in your shoes. By that, I mean that, as a copywriter, you should use first person when suggesting your reader to purchase something. For example, instead of having a button that says, "Subscribe Now," say something like, "Start My Free Trial".

When you're not putting the reader in your shoes, you should talk to them in the second person as if they're your sibling or significant other. Use "you" or "your" a lot. Don't be afraid to overuse these words.

Finally, when it comes to copywriting, you *should* break some rules of grammar. Your sentences need to make sense. They should still flow well. But it's OK to start sentences with conjunctions (like I started this sentence with "but") and end sentences with prepositions. Short, choppy, simple sentences are fine. Write like you're speaking to someone close to you... in an open, casual and fluid manner.

151

If you publish print content (or have a blog), your best pieces can be turned into landing pages by using the formatting guidelines I lay out in the next section and next chapter.

The best landing pages are your own best blog posts that you've already created. There's no need to go out and spend thousands of dollars to hire a copywriter to write a landing page, promotion, or order form.

Successful posts were successful for a reason. If people loved to read them as editorial, they'll still love to read them in copy format, even if the messaging is slightly different.

7 Ways To Present Copywriting To Improve Readability

Finally, make the readability of your words as simple to skim as possible.

Nowadays, it's rare for people to read anything word for word. A page with a bunch of words can be boring to look at.

There are ways you can convey your message by *highlighting* the big ideas in what you're saying. You want to make your words *visually pleasing* to the eye. This doesn't require much extra work on your end because you will have already written the copy.

1) **Bold key sentences**

2) ALL CAPS URGENT INFORMATION

3) Create lists or bullets to organize information

4) Italicize *side* comments

5) <u>Underline key ideas</u>

6) Highlight important sentences

7) Create separate sidebars or boxes for alternative topics that relate to your content

Why People Judge Pieces By Their Headlines Like People Judge Books By Their Front Covers

Headline writing is the first step to copy success. Headlines should include the themes and topics I list in this chapter.

Be creative with headlines. A headline isn't one phrase or sentence. It can have a pre-head before or above the main headline and then a subhead under that. Anticipate your customers' pains beforehand and provide an answer to those pains in the headline. Put as many key words as possible. Search engines will notice this and do free search engine optimization (SEO) for you.

Here's a sample headline I made up about a marketing podcast based on this book:

#1 Rated Marketing Podcast

FIFTY SHADES OF MARKETING RADIO

Listen And Learn The Best Marketing Practices In the 21st Century FREE… No Experience Required

This headline does the trick because it establishes credibility ("#1 Rated…"), gives the name of the product ("Fifty Shades Of Marketing Radio"), has a call to action ("Listen And Learn…"), and rids readers of their worry about not being advanced enough in marketing to listen to the podcast ("No Experience Required").

In general, numbers in headlines are good – i.e. "4 Ways To Improve Your Life", "10 Hacks To Get Free Airline Tickets", etc.

"How To" is also a great way to start a headline – i.e. "How To Get A Girlfriend", "How To Eat A Triple Pound Hotdog", etc.

You'll notice this book has a lot of chapter titles with numbers and "How To…" and "Why…"

E-MAIL SUBJECT LINES AND SOCIAL MEDIA COPY SHOULD BE WRITTEN LIKE YOU

WOULD WRITE HEADLINES. They follow the same rules.

7 Headline Formatting Rules To Follow

What the headline says is important, but what you say isn't the only element that will grab – and keep – readers' attentions.

For the best headline writing, follow these rules:

1) **Tahoma Red 36pt Bold with drop shadow and drop cap** – don't ask why… just do it. Research backs it up.

2) Centered

3) ALL CAPS

4) Use ellipses…

5) Don't use multiple full sentences.

6) Since you won't be using full sentences, don't use periods either – this will create a "stoppage in thinking" for your reader.

7) Use subheads… consider using pre-heads.

Chapter 19:
13 ELEMENTS OF LANDING PAGES PEOPLE WANT TO SEE

I've tested countless landing pages... fonts, colors, words, etc. I could talk about what didn't work... but that won't do you any good.

So below are "hacks" that have worked for me. I won't give any explanations. I'll tell you what's worked.

I'll leave the decision to you on whether you want to run with this info...

These tips are for general landing page copy. If you want to know how to handle headlines, then read the previous chapter on headlines.

1) **Background** – Blue or white... should be clear

2) **Font** – Arial

3) **Scrolling** – The less users have to scroll to find the important call to action, the better.

4) **Evidence** – Charts, poll results, data, research, statistics

5) **Trust Badges** – Seals showing satisfaction (or a "Staff Pick" or something "New"); write copy saying you won't spam them: "We won't ever sell your information to third-party sites."

6) **Bullet Points** – Lists are always better than jumbled words.

7) **Testimonials / Media Mentions** – You can pump yourself up as much as you want... but what other people say about you is more important than whatever you think of yourself. Including logos or quotes of media or reviewers who have featured you is a great way to build credibility.

8) **3D Product Image** – 3D images of your product type enhance your marketing. The image doesn't have to be your exact product. In fact, it shouldn't. Let's say you're giving away a free audio file of a lecture. You're obviously not

going to have a physical image of an audio file. So it's OK to use an image of a CD cover.

9) **Urgency** – Speed up actions by creating suspense or stressing limited time or availability. You can even lower your prices during a special period to add more urgency.

10) **Savings** – If you're selling a product, always compare a crossed out regular price to the discounted sales price, particularly in the "Buy Now" or "Add To Cart" button of your sales landing page. Show off that your discount is AMAZING. Discount at least 50%, and publicize it. So if you're selling a product for $100, say that the original price was $250 or something of that sort.

11) **First Person Purchase** – Use first person when suggesting that your reader should purchase something. For example, instead of having a button that says, "Subscribe Now," say something like, "Start My Free Trial".

12) **Call To Action Button** – Orange color

13) **One-click Purchasing for Existing Customers** – Filling out order forms is a tedious task. Most people get discouraged when they see long order forms that ask for so much information. For your existing customers, integrate a "one-click" purchasing button. You will see a minor bump in sales because of the ease of consumerism.

Landing Page Copy

If you publish print content (or have a blog), your best pieces can be turned into landing pages by using the formatting guidelines I lay out in the next section and next chapter.

The best landing pages are your own best blog posts that you've already created. There's no need to go out and spend thousands of dollars to hire a copywriter to write a landing page, promotion, or order form.

Successful posts were successful for a reason. If people loved to read them as editorial, they'll still love to read them in copy format, even if the messaging is slightly different.

Landing Page Resource

LeadPages – www.leadpages.net

LeadPages is a monthly subscription service that provides designed templates for landing pages of all kinds: lead generation, squeeze pages, order forms (long and short), shopping carts, webinars, and more. If you don't want to pay a web designer or developer for thousands of dollars a month, then LeadPages is your solution… for the low cost of $40 a month with the Pro Annual package (which I recommend over the $25 Standard package, which doesn't come with as many useful features).

LeadPages is valuable because it provides *proven* templates that convert. It has tens of thousands of paying subscribers, and it's able to track how well every one of their customers' campaigns do. Hence, it's able to recommend the *best* landing pages to customers to maximize their conversion rates.

The first 30 days are free, so if you don't like it within that timeframe, you can cancel your subscription and not pay anything.

Chapter 20:
4 REASONS WHY PUBLISHING A BOOK WILL MARKET YOU FOREVER

The book publishing industry has changed tremendously because of self-publishing. Amazon has overtaken traditional publishing houses and allowed anyone to become authors and distribute their works on its platform. Self-publishers can now also distribute their work to iTunes, iBooks and Audible.

Before getting into the benefits of book publishing, let me explain why traditional publishers are not as effective as they used to be…

Traditional publishers are still stuck in the 20th century ways of doing business. They don't understand the 21st century, New PR. They offer services that anyone can now emulate. And worst of all, they have a minimum length requirement of about 250, double-spaced Microsoft Word pages. Why is this length so stringent? Because 250 pages will ensure the book will be thick enough for text to print on the *spines* of hardback and paperback books at bookstores. If your book can't meet this requirement, then traditional publishers won't even read your book title.

The only problem with a 250-page, fundamental requirement of traditional publishers is that bookstores are dying. Borders went bankrupt. Barnes & Noble is closing stores by the month. And this is largely because:

a. It's easier for people to shop online on Amazon instead of visiting a physical store.

b. Self-publishing has allowed authors to publish directly to large online marketplaces.

To put it another way: the spines of books are now irrelevant, which means the length of any published book is now negligible.

There is no minimum length to *self-published* books. There are people – like Kamal Ravikant – who have written small books a little over 5,000 words and sold tens of thousands of copies.

Nevertheless, a lot of work is required to write and self-publish a book. It can take years for someone to do it themselves or tens of thousands of dollars to outsource it all (including the writing).

Books are still the fundamental building blocks to education. When we're little, our parents and teachers *make* us read. As we get older, the reading becomes copious thanks to textbooks.

Here's what writing a book can do for you:

1) Branding

People still judge books by their front covers, so seeing your name and book on major platforms like Amazon, iTunes and iBooks builds enormous credibility. People may not buy or read the book, but they will forever place you positively and authoritatively.

Over the long haul, this is great for your brand. You can leverage your brand to get you more business through speaking, consulting, new business opportunities, and more.

2) Establishes You As A Thought-Leader

Books carry knowledge, and knowledge gives us power. So the people who write books not only have knowledge, but society also views them as powerful figures... not just in their field, but also in society as a whole. Noble authors command a lot of respect from the public because of the emphasis on education worldwide.

3) Lead-Generation

Outside of becoming a powerful and respectable authority figure, authors can funnel in readers as leads to their businesses. If you offer something of value to anyone, they will reciprocate and give you value back. It's only human nature.

4) Pass-Along Effect

The greatness of books is that they don't disappear. Some of the great classics we read in high school have survived over the course of centuries. So even if your book doesn't receive good reviews or sell any copies today, it can still become a hit 20 or 200 years down the road. If you're alive to see this, great. If not, then your lineage can reap the benefits... or, if you leave a business behind, then it can benefit.

Chapter 21:
HOW TO PUBLISH A BOOK

I f you can't write, or if you don't like to write, then don't force yourself to do it. It takes a bit of passion to write even the simplest of sentences.

Writing and publishing a book can be a brutal process. As a published author, I've spent countless months banging my head against my desk.

But at the end of it all, it'll be worth it.

The first step in publishing a book is writing something with a clear focus and expertise. The narrower the topic, the better.

This book you're currently reading, for example, is about marketing principles in the digital age. That's niche. I could've written about my life story (I'm not sure what my life story is. It could be about studying, working, girls, basketball, my family, or one of a 100 other topics).

Don't be afraid to share your full insights and secrets. Many people are afraid of giving away ideas, but you'll be surprised at how rare it is for readers to *steal* your ideas and screw you. In my experience, I've gotten way more opportunities because I gave away my ideas than I have infringement cases. I haven't gone after anyone for plagiarizing my thoughts to date. Just as a parent is the only person who can parent his/her child, generally, so too the parent of an idea is the only person who can parent his/her idea.

After deciding the topic, someone needs to write. There are several strategies to do this. I prefer to write everything myself. I want to come across as genuine, and I also want my effort to show in every element of the book.

Other people may not have time to write... so they can get transcribers to ask them questions and then transcribe their answers. Then, they can send the transcription to an editor, who would make the sentences and paragraphs flow logically. Although this could cost five-figures if done with high quality, it is quick and efficient for businesses or people who don't have time but have money to spend. But again, I personally like to have control over what I write and how I say things. I like to get things started on paper. An editor can then edit my stuff to improve my writing and ideas.

Alternatively, you can use a transcription software to record yourself talking in front of your computer. Here are three I'd recommend. They all come with free versions or free trials:

http://www.nch.com.au/scribe/
https://www.audiotranskription.de/english
https://www.inqscribe.com/

Once you transcribe everything you need, then you can outsource the editing to turn your transcriptions into a book.

This is probably the easiest way to write a book with minimal effort.

Book Publishing Resources

Once the manuscript is complete, go to www.upwork.com or www.fiverr.com to find contractors who will design your front, back and spine covers as well as format your Kindle and paperback versions.

Go to www.acx.com to find someone to narrate your audiobook.

You can publish your paperback through www.createspace.com.

Kindle can be published through kdp.amazon.com.

E-books are very effective forms of content marketing if done correctly. Audiobooks and paperbacks are effective and need to be available on Amazon too. Making your book available in different forms increases the chances of people finding your book, thus resulting in more sales.

I love to write. People who don't like to write should still publish books to get their names out there and build their brands and clientele.

7 Keys To Book Marketing

This chapter will be quick to get you started. I won't completely walk you through the process because my next book will be all about book writing, publishing and marketing... so stay tuned for that by subscribing to my newsletter at www.nareshvissa.com.

1. When I published my previous #1 bestselling book Podcastnomics, I ran test campaigns **to give my book away for free for a limited period of time. I also ran discounted promotions** to sell the book.

2. **DO NOT PERMANANENTLY GIVE AWAY FREE BOOKS ON AMAZON**. Free books on Amazon carry little value to consumers. Pricing an e-book or Kindle at $2.99 is more effective than giving it away for free. Putting a price tag on something builds its value.

3. **If you have a following, then encourage your fans to write reviews on Amazon**. You don't have to force them to right five-star

reviews, but if you encourage your supporters to write reviews, there's a good chance they'll be writing five-star reviews anyway.

4. **Amazon gives people and products tremendous credibility**. I have seen what iTunes can do to a podcast's listenership and sales. Amazon can have the same impact on a brand new segment – a digitally oriented, more qualified segment – you may not be penetrating. These NEW people will *find you.*

5. **I used key words in my titles to target readers**. I also advertised on and rented e-mail lists, did Reddit AMAs, and marketed on social media.

6. **Include one testimonial snippet from a big-name expert on the front cover and two or three testimonials from experts on the back cover**. This adds mainstream credibility. As much as you shouldn't judge a book by its front cover, the fact of the matter is that it's only human nature to do so.

7. **Make the entire first chapter readily viewable online or downloadable free of charge**. This will be a great opportunity to plug your websites, products, and anything else that can improve lead-generation, since the "free sample" of your book will display them.

The writing process, from beginning to end, can take years. The publishing and marketing process, from beginning to end, can take up to six months.

To fully self-publish and market, it costs a minimum of about $300 per book (not including time).

But the results have been worthwhile for me. I've gotten many new clients and partnership deals thanks to my books.

I could write 15,000 more words on this topic, so that's why my next book will be all about writing, self-publishing and marketing books. My last book hit #1 on the Amazon Bestseller list. I've figured out a formula that will lay out – step by step – how anyone can become a successful author. And if your book sells enough copies, large, traditional publishers will want to buy the rights to your book. That's what happened to <u>Fifty Shades of Grey</u> author E.L. James.

If you're interested in my next book on self-publishing, then subscribe free to my newsletter/mailing list by visiting www.nareshvissa.com.

If you're ready to publish a book and need immediate help on how to do it, don't hesitate to reach out to me at Naresh dot Vissa at Gmail dot com.

Chapter 22:
THE POWER OF PODCASTING

*N*ote: *This is a snippet on podcasting. For an even more thorough explanation of how you can start your podcast – from soup to nuts – you'll want to check out my previous book Podcastnomics, which hit #1 on Amazon's bestseller list. It's available on Amazon in Kindle, paperback and audiobook.*

Podcasting is an incredibly niche area of media production, online marketing and sales strategy. Talk to marketing directors at most companies, and it's likely they'll know little to nothing about podcasting and its benefits in improving a firm's brand, publicity, awareness, goodwill and overall sales.

Podcasting isn't a new phenomenon, but it hasn't caught on to the mainstream quite yet. For example, in the HBO series *The Newsroom*, AWM (Atlantis World Media) CEO Leona Lansing (Jane Fonda) threatens to fire anchor Will McAvoy (Jeff Daniels) by saying he is one strike away from hosting his own podcast, as if it's some sort of insult.

Having worked on podcasts for many years now, I can say that companies and larger corporations don't see –

or know – the value of podcasts yet. It's an easy way to build an audience and engage with it.

This presents a tremendous opportunity.

If AWM released more content in podcast format, AWM wouldn't have faced such budgetary constraints.

How iTunes Created The Podcasting Industry

The idea of podcasting isn't anything revolutionary. A podcast is essentially a radio show. Nothing groundbreaking there.

BUT THE ONLY REASON WHY PODCASTING IS A VENTURE WORTH PURSUING FOR BUSINESSES IS ITUNES.

iTunes has changed the game. Apple has spent a lot of money and resources to create a podcast functionality, and in return, podcasting has turned into a profitable and worthwhile venture. iTunes' podcasting platform makes Apple a lot of money.

iTunes allows podcasters to get out in front of the world... like Amazon allows authors to sell their books.

This means, as a business owner, you have access to a very large audience – and potential customers!

How Apple Is Helping Podcasters Get Leads

Why is iTunes so big for podcasting? Think about it...

Think about all the people who own an iPhone or iPad or Mac... really any Apple product. And then realize that the "Podcasts" app automatically comes hard-coded with all of these products.

The new iOS integrates the Podcast app natively onto Apple products. This will be the turning point for podcasting. Hundreds of millions of people will be getting this app around the globe, and they won't be able to delete it.

Will every Apple user use the "Podcasts" app? No. But already, Apple is helping market its podcasting platform to the masses.

Now, think about the types of people who own Apple products. We're talking about folks who have some tech savvy and money to spend.

The moment a user "Subscribes" to a podcast on iTunes, he/she has committed to receive all of a podcast's episodes indefinitely. This means they actually *want* to listen to every show. And it means this user is highly qualified. They're likely educated, working-class or studying, and have money to spend to improve themselves.

THIS IS THE ULTIMATE LEAD. NO OTHER MARKETING CHANNEL WILL PROVIDE HIGHER QUALITY LEADS.

In essence, Apple already does the filtering for podcasters. It's up to you to come out with consistent and quality content and distribute it effectively.

Podcast Trends

Podcasts can be listened to anywhere... at the gym or in the office, while cooking or traveling by car, train or plane, etc.

Content marketers are on the edge of an inflection point in podcasting. There are now close to a billion people with the Podcasts app on their iOS devices, and that is just on the iOS side.

That's a big market. Podcasting is now entering into its true golden age of mass adoption.

What Should My Podcast Be About?

The first step to have a successful podcast is picking the proper niche. This is integral. The more targeted the niche, the better.

For example, I met someone a few months ago who's an expert in fixing cars (mechanical problems, tires, paint, etc.). I suggested that he come out with a car mechanics show. Every episode could focus on a specific car issue. He could share all his wisdom.

Put yourself in this guy's shoes...

I searched iTunes and the Internet for "car mechanics" podcasts. About ten shows came up. This isn't great news, but there's still an opportunity here. You can do a better job of providing timelier and better content and steal market share.

You can interview car mechanic experts on your show... go to Amazon's "Books" section and search for "car mechanic." Hundreds of books pop up. Contact those authors and ask them to be guests on your show.

You can answer questions from listeners who are experiencing issues with their cars. This will help them save money! People love to save money! Especially on their cars. Most mechanics around the corner know the average person knows nothing about cars. So they make their money by scamming customers. I know I'm not the only one who's gotten scammed by a mechanic!

There are many opportunities like this. Once you build your audience and platform, you can start monetizing: get people to come to your shop to get their car fixed... or incorporate advertising, affiliate marketing, paid (subscription) content, selling your consulting services, selling your car mechanic products, speaking gigs, writing a book, etc.

4 Ways To Use Podcasts To Grow Your Business

A radio show with 1,000 listeners is pathetic... because terrestrial radio is a medium with a passive audience.

So it would make sense to think that a podcast with 1,000 listeners would be pathetic too. But the difference is that podcast audiences are *active*... not passive.

To put it in simpler terms...

Imagine giving a speech to 1,000 attendees in a private auditorium. That's what it's like to podcast to an audience of 1,000 listeners. They're all listening to you.

As a result, podcasts are a good way to build a following, and ultimately, a customer base. It is great for funneling in leads so you can sell them something.

You can sell:

- Whatever your business offers

- Books

- Consulting services

- Other people's products (if you work out a deal for them to pay you)

Here are four ways you can sell your products or services through your own podcast:

1) **Send a sales e-mail to your podcast mailing list.**

   Popular sales blog *Yesware* says that an e-mail loses its gleam after 24 hours, so e-mailing your mailing list is the quickest and most direct way to make a buck. You will see action taken and sales pour in immediately.

2) **Post links to your products on your episode page and social media.**

   Your episode page has a pass-along effect. People will be able to find your site years down the road. This means there's always a chance your product will be sold in perpetuity.

3) **Have banners marketing your product on your podcast site.**

   The banners can take clickers straight to a product overview page with a short order form.

4) **Create a vanity URL to plug on the podcast so you can sell a product and track sales.**

   Announce the URL on-air so listeners have a clear call to action. The vanity URL can host a short order form or longer promotional copy to sell whatever product you'd like.

If you'd like a full guide on how you can start your podcast, check out my book <u>Podcastnomics</u> – available on Amazon in Kindle, paperback and audiobook.

Why Podcast Marketing Is Trumping Traditional PR And Marketing

As I mentioned earlier, having a podcast with 1,000 listeners is equivalent to giving a speech to 1,000 attendees in a private auditorium. Consequently, not just hosts stand to benefit from podcasting. Guests on podcasts have a great opportunity to sell themselves and their products too. Podcasts are always looking for good guests – thought leaders, authors, executives, and creative visionaries. So if you or your business has something of unique value to offer, then go to iTunes and search for podcasts you think you'd be a good guest on!

For authors, the podcast tour has replaced the book tour. It's no longer necessary to travel around the world to meet readers and autograph books. Authors can instead hold webinars or do a bunch of podcast interviews to get the word out and then forward folks to Amazon to buy their books… from their home and in their pajamas!

Chapter 23:
HOW VIDEO MARKETING CAN SELL YOUR PRODUCTS AND BRANDS

Videos are visual. In today's print content oversaturation, video can clearly distinguish itself from the fluff... and the numbers prove it.

Digital video ads are quickly becoming more effective than traditional TV ads. *eMarketer* found that 75% of ad agency executives agree that digital video ads have equal or greater impact than display and TV ads. By 2017, Bloomberg researchers expect global consumer video activity to represent nearly 70 percent of all consumer Internet traffic, up from 57 percent in 2012. Nielsen found that 18-34 year-olds are watching 53% more online video. The 35-49 age group is watching 80% more online video. This means Internet users will be exposed to more video in the future.

Marketers and entrepreneurs can't ignore this trend anymore, especially since it's gotten so cheap to produce video content.

Every brand and product needs a video to support and explain itself. The video can be as short as one minute or as long as one hour. Both lengths have proven to be effective at sales conversion and brand loyalty… though the more value you can deliver in the video, the better.

Video discourages many marketers and entrepreneurs because they think they need to hire an expensive Hollywood producer to release something of high value. With the advances in digital freelancers and cheap contract workers, that is no longer true.

The definition of "high value" has also evolved with the digital space. No longer does something need to be Academy Award-winning to be respectable or convincing.

My first exposure to video marketing came when I came across one of the top financial publishers and online marketers in the world: Stansberry & Associates Investment Research. This was in 2011, when Stansberry released a viral PowerPoint-type of narration to convince people to buy their top entry-level newsletter research product. "End of America" is the video. It's over an hour long, consisting mostly of text on a screen and a narrator reading that text. You can view the full video by going on YouTube and searching "Stansberry End of America" to see what I'm talking about.

The "End of America" video became one of the most successful sales videos of all time. The fiscally conservative passed it around and generated hundreds of thousands of brand new, paying customers for Stansberry.

"End of America" goes to show the power of video marketing and that the fundamentals of a good message matter… not the production quality.

Video Ideas

The video should convince people to like you or your product. It can be about anything...

- Interview with or monologue by the CEO

- PowerPoint-type presentation that mostly transcribes text of the narrator's voice

- Whiteboard animation with narrator – search for "whiteboard animation" on YouTube to see examples. These animations can be put together through www.fiverr.com or www.upwork.com (formerly Elance/oDesk) for about $10-15 per minute.

- Customer, client, partner or media testimonials

- Image-based overview slideshow

- Something incredibly high quality that'll require heavy research, travel, writing, reporting, or editing

Don't forget about the most important element of your video:

The Call To Action

A call to action (CTA) is an instruction to elicit an immediate response. Examples of CTAs include:

> "Go to www.xyz.com to learn more."

> "Buy stock in Vissa Enterprises today by logging into your brokerage account and entering the symbol VISS."

> "Enter your e-mail address in the opt-in box below to receive your coupon for 20% off your next purchase."

The video needs to integrate calls to actions throughout, but the CTAs need to be repeated multiple times at the end of any video so viewers are left with clear instructions on what they should do to take advantage of a great product or offer.

YouTube allows publishers to place overlay advertisements with external link annotations within their videos. For example, if you want users to buy a product, then you can create an overlay ad that says something like, "Click here to purchase now." This dynamic approach allows you to time exactly when you'd like this ad to pop up. Google AdWords runs these campaigns, so YouTube will charge you per click. You must have a Google AdWords account and have it connected to your YouTube to execute these overlay add campaigns.

Here's how you can create your YouTube overlay advertisement:

1. Create a Google AdWords account with your same YouTube username or ID (or connect your AdWords account to your YouTube ID).

2. Sign in to your YouTube account.

3. At the top of your Dashboard, click "Account".

4. Under My Videos, click "Uploaded Videos".

5. Click "Edit" next to the video you'd like to place an overlay ad.

6. Find the "Call-To-Action Overlay" section and fill out the required fields.

How Can You Produce A Video At A Low Cost?

Go to www.upwork.com or www.fiverr.com and search for video specialists or animators. You'll find tons of qualified and experienced professionals who will charge you anywhere from $50-$100 per five minutes of full production.

There will be some work required on your end. Most of these people who charge such low prices live overseas, so their English isn't very good. You must provide clear instructions and direction to make the project go as smoothly as possible. You will need to do the grunt work yourself – providing all the necessary elements like pictures and testimonials, recording an mp3 of any narration, writing the script, etc. That should take a few hours on your end, but the rest can be outsourced.

3 Locations To Place Your Video

Once the video is complete, you can host it on YouTube and embed it on your website. I recommend YouTube over other services like Amazon, Adobe Flash, QuickTime and Vimeo because the video will have a greater chance of getting more views or going viral because of YouTube's high search engine optimization (since it's owned by Google) and high traffic (it's the second largest search engine in the world). It's free to use and supports most video formats.

The video should be compatible across all devices and function consistently… not just desktops and laptops, but mobile and tablet too.

There are various places you can post your video on your site, and I've mentioned some in the coming paragraphs… just make sure it's always placed on the top of any page! Placing it elsewhere will make it difficult for people to find.

1) Homepage

Make the video the first item a visitor views. This will get people familiar with you and your products and services before they start clicking around.

2) Top of promotional page

If you're looking to get more subscribers to your mailing list or want to market a special event you're having and want people to show up, then on top of all your promotional copy, paste your video. Users can watch the video first and then read everything else you have below it... just don't forget to have your call to action buttons below the video and again below your marketing copy! You don't want your viewers to have to scroll all the way down to the bottom to find your call to action buttons. Make it easy for them to find the buttons.

3) Top of order form

If you're selling a product, then have a video at the top – front and center, above and before any promotional or shopping cart information. Very few people blindly buy anything. Online buyers want to make the most informed decision possible before pulling out their credit cards and purchasing something. Your video will help with that. But again... don't forget to have your call to action buttons below the video and again below your sales copy! You don't want your viewers to have to scroll all the way down to the bottom to find your call to action buttons. Make it easy for them to find the buttons.

5 Optimization Must-Haves For Video

When you upload your video to YouTube, you want to make sure you optimize your setup thoroughly. Here are five areas you should pay attention to:

1) Title

Put the most important words in your title. Write your title similarly to how you'd write print headlines.

2) Keywords in description

Make the description as thorough as possible. Long descriptions are OK. Remember that most users will only watch your video and may not even make it to your description section... but the content in your description will optimize your video positively.

3) Tags

Many rookie video publishers upload their video but neglect to fill out all necessary fields. Make sure you fill out the "Tags" section with any relevant keywords so your video has the greatest shot at being discovered through search.

4) Frequent content (if you have a YouTube channel or video blog/vlog)

If you're making one video to sell a product or raise awareness on a subject, then you likely won't be pursuing a full YouTube channel or video blog (vlog) strategy. But if you want to come out with regular videos for training or editorial purposes, then you must be consistent in releasing your content.

Let's say, for example, that you come out with one crappy video. Now you're stuck with one crappy video as your brand. But if you release ten videos, and nine are crappy, but one is amazing, then that one video will be enough to brand you well. It will also pump up the views for your other videos, thus making them less crappy.

There is no set formula on how much content you should generate, but know that you should be releasing something every week at the minimum (if you want to go full steam on establishing yourself as a video publisher).

5) Enable comments

Comments improve SEO and lets YouTube know that your video is relevant and engaging. YouTube can then suggest it to viewers of other similar videos and bump it up search results.

Never disable your comments! Doing so comes across as cowardly!

Video Resource – How To Drive Up Your Video Views

www.ShareYouTubeVideos.com

Consider driving up – and *buying* – views to your YouTube videos through Share YouTube Videos (SYV). The pricing is approximately $1 per 1,000 views you buy.

This site drives *organic* traffic to videos. It doesn't use black hat marketing techniques. If it did, then it would've been shut down years ago. Instead, it's been around for nearly a decade (as of October 2015). It follows all Internet laws and YouTube's terms and services. Even better, ShareYouTubeVideos.com has a good customer service team that honors requests and complaints in a timely fashion.

Six-figure views automatically grab people's attention. It'll get people interested to watch: "Why does this video have 110,000 views? It must be good," is the average human's thought-process. It's a good way to market your video.

Getting even 1,000 views on YouTube is a challenge. I have eight-year-old videos on my YouTube channel that haven't cracked 500 views. ShareYouTubeVideos.com is your chance to instantly shoot your video to the top and become an authoritative leader.

Not only can you buy views on ShareYouTubeVideos.com, but you can also buy comments, shares, likes, favorites, subscribers, and more.

Video Marketing Wrap-up

The fundamentals in this book are still important – writing good copy, producing high-quality design and compelling content, great customer service, etc.

But every marketer or entrepreneur should use video to increase its respective brand and sales conversion. Because video production costs are so low now, there is no reason not to. The financial risk has been eliminated.

If you need help with getting started on your videos, don't hesitate to contact me at naresh dot vissa at gmail dot com.

NARESH VISSA

Chapter 24:
8 REASONS AND DIGITAL WAYS TO LEVERAGE PUBLIC SPEAKING

Whether it's at a conference, seminar, live media interview, press conference, online presentation, webinar or talking to a classroom full of students, speaking engagements are great ways to make your voice heard in front of many people at once. Here's why:

1) **You become an authority figure literally standing on a pedestal**

   It's a privilege to be given a room full of hungry learners and to feed them whatever you'd like.

   If you are new to the speaking circuit and have to pay your way to speak – meaning, you're not being paid to speak and have to cover travel, lodging, food expenses – it's still worth it. Speaking to groups of qualified people allows you to:

2) **Put yourself out there**

   You can go from nobody to somebody by giving a solid presentation. Speaking gives you an opportunity for your 45 minutes of fame.

Nobody knew who Barack Obama was during the 90's. The Bushs and Clintons ruled politics, along with status quo guys like Ted Kennedy, Al Gore, Bob Dole and Newt Gingrich.

But Obama gave an uplifting speech at the 2004 Democratic National Convention. It went viral on YouTube, which had just hit mainstream Internet users.

The success of that one speech led Obama's books to become #1 bestsellers, which in turn helped him run for President of the United States in 2008.

The rest is history. No 2004 DNC speech = no Presidency for Obama in 2008.

3) Good practice for the next gig

Speaking gigs have a compounding effect. You do one that leads to another that leads to another and so on.

The only way you get better at speaking is through practice in real-life situations. And the only way you can practice real-life situations is by speaking more and more.

You have to start somewhere. By the time you hit the big circuits, you will have gotten the fears, pains, and embarrassments out of your system.

4) Quality audiences

The people attending professional events are not uneducated party animals looking to hook up. That's what clubs are for.

Attendees are there because they are enthusiastic about the subject matter. They are very qualified. They gave up time and money to attend and listen to you.

So they'll pay attention to you... and if they like you, they'll become your biggest fans and customers.

It's very hard to find your target audience from your home or office. But if you're speaking at an event, your target audience is already right there in front of you. The event planners did all the work. All you have to do is show up and put on a show.

For the actual content of the presentation itself...

5) Seek digital venues over physical ones

When I first got started in the speaking circuit, I flew to St. Louis to give a seminar on podcasting. I paid for airfare, food and lodging. The two-day trip cost more than $500.

A month later, I gave the exact same presentation on podcasting at a virtual summit/conference... meaning it was all online. I didn't travel anywhere... no flights, hotels or anything. I simply recorded myself giving the PowerPoint presentation on my computer and sent it to the summit organizers a week before the event.

The virtual summit produced four times (4x!) as many leads than what I got when I went to St. Louis!

Why?

Because people can attend virtual summits from anywhere. They don't have to go through the financial and logistical hassles of getting to a physical location. They can participate at home, work, on vacation, etc.

People can also view virtual presentations at any time. Virtual presentations can be archived so people in the future can go back to watch them. I still have leads coming in from that virtual summit presentation I gave a year ago!

6) Don't create a long, boring PowerPoint deck with a bunch of words and numbers

Too many professional presentations have a lot of text as bullets and numbers. Even worse, bad presenters have a bad habit of reading all these words and numbers directly from their slides. If you're going to read or make your audience read all this stuff during your presentation, then they'll stop listening to you and get lost in the shuffle.

Once you lose your audience, you become a loser in their eyes.

The slides support what you say. So make them visually pleasing with pictures, innovative charts, and big ideas.

I even recommend that after creating your slide deck, you hire someone overseas to improve every single slide to make it more visually pleasing. To do this, go to www.fiverr.com and search for PowerPoint slide designers. The best ones will charge you $1-2 per slide. That's not pricy at all. I've never spent more than $20 on my PowerPoint enhancements. Doing this makes your presentation more professional and well done.

A great presentation is delivered formidably by the presenter... not by what's on the screen in front of the audience. Great presenters don't even need the visual aids to captivate the audience. In the end, it all comes back to the competency of the presenter.

Keep your slides simple and make them nice, but let your value do the talking.

7) Provide actionable steps and resources

As much as we say the opposite, people love being told what to do. They want immediate advice so they can get immediate results.

Slides with lists, "cheat sheets," resources (i.e. books, websites, etc.) are what get the audience to take notes and follow-up.

8) Give away something digitally

Many speakers give out physical products like thumb drives, pens, and notepads. There's no way to collect leads through these items.

That's why digital giveaways are great lead generators. If you have a book or special report, then create a vanity URL with a squeeze page to collect e-mails. You can tell your audience to visit the vanity URL to get your product FREE of charge. Put the URL up on a slide with the giveaway offer.

If you're too lazy to create a vanity URL to collect e-mails, then tell the audience to e-mail you "right now" so they can get the free giveaway and let them know that they'll be added to your free newsletter mailing list. That way, you can respond to each e-mail personally and follow-up in the future. They'll be in your database.

This is what I say to attendees to give away my product to collect leads:

"Everybody, you now have my permission to take out your phone. Take it out right now, and send me an e-mail to the address listed on the slide to get your free copy of xyz."

Best of luck, and may the force of speaking be with you.

Why Webinars Are Effective

Webinars are online seminars. Instead of reading the tone of a white paper or blog post, webinars allow attendees to see or hear the expert. In addition, webinars provide interactive experiences to build rapport quickly and expedite the sales process through a funnel. Attendees can directly ask the host questions by speaking into their microphones or typing in the discussion section of the webinar software. They can also speak to other attendees within this section.

The fast pace of webinars (45 minutes–1 hour) converts leads quicker than if they were to go through a traditional sales funnel, which could take months to execute. Leads can hang around and not make any decision until you force them to. Webinars are the perfect way to get your audience to act on the spot. Think of a webinar as an "in-person meeting" with that company you've wanted to work for your entire life. At the end of that meeting, the company will make a decision.

People can attend webinars from anywhere. They can participate at home, work, on vacation, etc. They don't have to go through the financial and logistical hassle of getting to a physical location, and the organizers don't have to deal with the organization and cost of babysitting attendees.

The post-webinar marketing makes webinars most effective though. If you decide to do a webinar, be sure you send follow-up sales e-mails to your attendees with info on how they can buy a product you plugged. I'd even go as far as hiring an outsourced telesales team who can call attendees on the phone and sell them on the product. This strategy of following up post-webinar – particularly on the phone – has proven to be incredibly effective for my clients.

Webinar Resources – How To Execute Your Webinar

The same principles on why people should publicly speak apply to webinars. You can use the slide deck of your presentation – live or taped (though live is highly recommended because it's more real).

To tape a webinar video, use Camtasia Studio to record yourself giving your presentation. Camtasia is FREE for 30 days and can be downloaded at www.techsmith.com/camtasia. It connects directly to PowerPoint so you can record easily. The software also allows you to easily pause during your presentation or edit at the end. You can export your final video as .mov or .mp4 files.

If you want to do a live webinar, then use InstantTeleseminar, which can be procured at www.instantteleseminar.com. It's one of the best webinar software that allows subscribers to integrate their marketing with solid lead generation and customer service.

Chapter 25:
THE NEW PR

Why Traditional PR Is A Scam

I'm a publicist. I represent clients in the financial and economic space. I've worked with tens of clients over the years. And despite making a good amount of money off publicizing my clients, I'll be the first person to "out" most PR firms as scams. They're not what they used to be, largely because publicists still market their clients the same way they did before the Internet economy. They charge insane amounts of money, and they know very little about the term "return on investment."

When I was an undergraduate student at Syracuse University's S.I. Newhouse School of Public Communications – one of the best journalism schools in the country according to NewsPro – a few of my journalism professors would tell the crappy journalists to drop their major from journalism to PR.

"If you can't handle the pressure of deadlines, brainstorming, shooting, editing, writing, and putting together a good story, then don't do this. Do PR," I remember one of my professors saying.

For a one-day media tour (meaning the client has 15-20 minute interviews lined up over a 6-8 hour window), PR firms can charge upwards of $20,000. Their monthly retainers range from $700 all the way to $25,000 (depending on the quality and experience of the publicist or firm), with a three-month minimum. I'm not making these numbers up. I recently had to put together a spreadsheet of PR firms' rates for a client of mine, and these staggering figures are the latest industry standards.

Is the cost worth it even if your publicist can get you on as a guest on CNN or FOX News? That's a subjective question. To me, it's not worth it... because, given today's digital age, traditional PR generates very little return. Any PR strategy now has to consider the Internet.

Will the live video hit be available for broadcast and archive online? Will the live radio interview be available in podcast format after? Does the newspaper have an online digital version so you can share it on social media?

When is the last time you watched or heard an interview on TV or in your car's radio and you said, "This author is awesome. I can't wait to go home and buy his book!" Chances are, you'll forget the guest's name, product and website within five minutes.

Consider the case of Greg Smith – an ex-Goldman Sachs institutional salesman. He wrote a tell-all book about life on Wall Street, titled <u>WHY I LEFT GOLDMAN SACHS: A Wall Street Story</u>.

Smith got a big publisher, the Hachette Book Group, to publicize his book. *60 Minutes* and the *New York Times* covered it in-depth. Smith did interviews on all the major media outlets. He got all the publicity in the world.

Despite all the hoopla, Smith sold barely 20,000 copies of his book. He would've been lucky to make six-figures in royalties. Hachette didn't even break-even on their $1.5 million advance to Smith.

The Greg Smith scenario is what so many business owners and marketers fall for. It's why the PR and branding professions are still in business.

Every person I know who's hired a PR firm on retainer has been ripped off – even by the firms who charge a measly $700 per month retainer. There are countless message board threads and blog posts online of folks who felt duped.

People should do their own publicity work. I don't expect Donald Trump or Mark Cuban to be their own publicists, but someone on their marketing team should do it. They shouldn't have to outsource PR to a firm. That's why, in this chapter, I'll teach you *how* YOU can be your own publicist.

4 Reasons Why Publicity Makes Business Sense

1) Free

You don't have to pay anything to get media publicity, whereas you have to pay to advertise anything anywhere.

2) Believable

Ads can be hyperbolic. They can lie or be misleading, and most people who are qualified to be buyers are smart enough to know this.

PR paints a better sense of you. It's more real.

3) Multiplier effect

You can do a media interview, and that can lead to more media interviews if content producers like you or what you have to say.

If you're good enough for a national publication, then you're good enough for small publications and speaking gigs. There won't be a charge to you.

You can come out with a good ad, but nobody will run your ad for free. There is no compounding of advertisements, unless it's a video produced in such a way on YouTube that people start sharing it with each other.

4) Separation from competition

A civil engineer who is sourced by *Popular Science* isn't just another civil engineer. He's now THE civil engineer. Not because he's the smartest or the best... but because he was featured in *Popular Science*. And thanks to that feature, it'll be easier for the Science Channel and *Business Insider* to interview him too.

The State Of Expert Sources

There's a large supply of expert sources. The problem is... most of these "expert" sources aren't high quality.

Media publications NEED high quality expert sources. There is a great demand for them.

Put simply: there is a large demand for GREAT expert sources. But there's an even LARGER supply of crappy experts. This supply of crappy experts far exceeds the demand for high quality experts.

So your challenge – as an entrepreneur, business owner or marketer – is to convince the media that you're a high quality expert. Media professionals look at the total package – not just your pitch, but also your background and accomplishments.

4 Ways To Build Your Online Authority

In the "new PR," experts need to build up their online presence. The first thing editors and producers will do is Google the name of the expert. They'll:

1) **Visit your website**.

   Have a nice website that makes you look good. Include a section with all your media hits and mentions. Include another section that has your bio and another section with your books (if you have any). On the front page of your site, highlight that you have been featured by the media in big lettering (if you have been): "AS SEEN ON [CNN, FOX NEWS, etc.]" or "FEATURED IN [*NEW YORK TIMES, USA TODAY*, etc.]. This will build up your reputation and add to your media experience and credibility. The media likes experts who are familiar and comfortable with being in front of a microphone or camera.

2) **Search Google News to see if other media have quoted or interviewed the expert**.

   One media hit will lead to another, which will lead to another and another. Being featured by the media should have a compounding effect. If members of the media can't find much on you through other media mentions, then they could write you off because you might be terrible in front of a microphone or camera.

If you have a popular full name like John Smith, James Johnson, Randy Miller, Brendan Jones, etc., then you MUST include a middle initial to distinguish yourself clearly on the Internet from the thousands of other people with your name. There's only one other Naresh Vissa in the world, so I don't need to worry about including a middle initial.

For instance, the actor Michael B. Jordan includes his middle initial to avoid confusion with the greatest basketball player of all time.

3) **Check Amazon to see if the expert has any books, and if so, how many reviews**.

If you haven't written a book yet, then definitely get on it. It establishes your expertise and gives the media a focused topic to discuss.

4) **Look at social media clout**.

The numbers of Facebook Likes and Twitter followers are key metrics with the media. Make sure you are active on all social media too (Instagram, Pinterest, LinkedIn, Myspace, Snapchat, etc.)!

Build up all of these and then leverage them in the pitch.

3 Resources To Get Media Interviews

To gain media presence, you have to start somewhere (small) with blogs and podcasts and work your way up to bigger media. It takes years… sometimes decades.

When I started out trying to get publicity, I represented myself because I had no money. I did not intend to spend $10,000-20,000 a month on a publicist.

I've gotten at least 50 media hits and mentions going all the way back to my college days. MSNBC, Bloomberg, *USA Today*, *Deseret News*, *Entrepreneur*, numerous podcasts and radio shows have featured me.

Here are some resources you can use to get cracking:

1) HARO (Help A Reporter Out)

HARO (Help A Reporter Out) is a platform that connects content producers (editors, producers, reporters, etc.) with sources. It sends out three e-mails a day – one in the early morning, one in the early afternoon, and one in the evening – with up to 50 queries *from journalists* (not publicists) who give an overview of the stories they're working on and the sources they need.

To get expert requests delivered straight to your e-mail inbox, you can join HARO at www.HelpAReporter.com completely free of charge. Once you start receiving the regular e-mail newsletter, seek niche queries that you qualify for. For example, if you see a query that is "Seeking Successful Entrepreneurs," then that's not very niche. There are hundreds of thousands of successful entrepreneurs around the world. If you respond to that query, then you'll be competing against the likes of Bill Gates and Oprah Winfrey. So don't even bother wasting your time by responding to those broad queries.

However, if you see a niche query you'd be a good fit for, then respond to it using the techniques I laid out on how to pitch the media. Let's say you're a private and independent stripper (so you only service parties, webcams – not clubs), and you find a query on HARO where a journalist is looking to interview a stripper... then you can respond back to the query with your pitch on who you are, and it will then be delivered to the journalist's inbox. Bill Gates and Oprah can't compete with that!

An hour after posting one query, the journalist can receive up to a hundred e-mails back from assistants, marketing assistants, publicists, and experts, so your pitch MUST stand out from the crowd using the recipe I lay out on pitching coming up.

I've gotten at least 50 media hits and mentions going all the way back to my college days, mostly due to my activity on HARO. MSNBC, Bloomberg, *USA Today*, *Deseret News*, *Entrepreneur*, numerous podcasts and radio shows: I've been around the circuit. I've read every e-mail and query HARO has sent for nearly ten years, and I haven't paid a dime for any of the publicity I've received.

2) RadioGuestList.com

Similar to HARO is Radio Guest List (www.RadioGuestList.com), except Radio Guest List sends one e-mail every two days or so, and each e-mail has only three or four queries. Furthermore, Radio Guest List only sends out radio and podcast queries. It's free to use.

3) iTunes

Doing podcast interviews that are published on iTunes is well worth your time. Here's why…

Podcasts will be on iTunes forever. They have a pass-along effect and long shelf life. A century from now, the mp3s will still be available for download. This is the greatness of podcasts on iTunes over terrestrial radio. Terrestrial radio shows air live and then disappear.

Think about all the people who own an iPhone or iPad or Mac... really any Apple product. And then realize that the "Podcasts" app automatically comes with all of these products.

The latest iOS updates integrate the Podcasts app natively onto Apple products. That means more than a billion people get the Podcasts app around the globe.

Does every Apple user use the "Podcasts" app? No. But iTunes has crossed more than a billion podcast downloads, and that number is growing rapidly. There are also now more than 200,000 podcasts on iTunes too. With so many podcasts come great opportunities for expert interviews.

Now, think about the types of people who own Apple products... we're talking about folks who have some tech savvy and money to spend.

The moment a user "Subscribes" to a podcast on iTunes, they have committed to receive all of a podcast's episodes indefinitely. This means they actually *want* to listen to every show. And it means this user is highly qualified. They're likely educated, working-class or studying, and have money to spend to improve themselves.

THIS IS THE ULTIMATE LEAD. NO OTHER MARKETING CHANNEL WILL PROVIDE HIGHER QUALITY LEADS.

In essence, Apple already does the filtering for podcasters. So, as a guest on a podcast, you'll be exposed to a very qualified audience.

Being a guest on a podcast with 1,000 listeners is equivalent to giving a speech to 1,000 attendees in a private auditorium. Consequently, it's not just hosts who stand to benefit from podcasting. Guests on podcasts have a great opportunity to sell themselves and their products too. Podcasts are always looking for good guests – thought leaders, authors, executives, and creative visionaries.

For authors, the podcast tour has replaced the book tour. It's no longer necessary to travel around the world to meet readers and autograph books. Authors can instead hold webinars or do a bunch of podcast interviews to get the word out and then forward folks to Amazon to buy their books… from their home and in their pajamas!

If you or your business has something of unique value to offer, then go to iTunes and search for podcasts you think you'd be a good guest on. To find podcasts to pitch yourself on, open the Podcasts app on your iOS device or the Podcasts section in iTunes, and search your expertise. If your niche is running, then type in "running" or "marathon training." If your niche is "stripping," then type in "stripping." See what pops up. If there are podcast shows in your niche, then contact those shows and pitch yourself. You can get the website of the show through its iTunes page. If it's not provided, then Google the show or the name of the host to find contact info.

Note: BlogTalkRadio is a competitor to iTunes and has many shows too. The quality of listeners and return on BlogTalkRadio is not as strong though. You can apply the same principles I laid out on getting iTunes podcast interviews to BlogTalkRadio.

5 Steps To Pitch The Media

There's no way you're getting publicity without trying. If you're a small business or start-up entrepreneur, you'll need to learn how to get in touch with media and get them to be interested in your story.

Here are some steps:

1) E-MAIL the editor/producer

More media professionals want to be e-mailed rather than called. Phone is disappearing as a way of doing business – for better or for worse.

I get annoyed when publicists or experts call me at random times of the day asking if I can book them for an interview on one of the podcasts or publications I manage.

E-mail your pitch. If you don't hear back, then follow-up a few days later.

2) Enticing subject line

The most important part of your e-mail pitch is your subject line. It's what gets people to open up your message. It needs to be a shocking, controversial, newsworthy or problem-solving hook.

3) Address the receiver

Make sure you call – by name – who your pitch is to. Include the person's first name. Don't send out a mass e-mail that says, "Dear Reporter,".

This adds a personal touch to your pitch. If you don't know the name of the person, then a,

"Dear Reporter," or "Dear Producer," is OK. It's better than nothing.

4) **Explain how you fit into the mission of the show or publication**

If the medium you're pitching is about online dating, then start off by establishing yourself as an online dating expert. Include hyperlinks to your books, talk about your history – i.e. awards you've been given and accomplishments. On your website, you should have a media section that includes links to all your previous media interviews, so include the link to your media page so the content producer can see, listen or watch your established media presence.

5) **Only at the end of the pitch do you "make the sale"**

Include your contact information. Tell them you're available to discuss more.

In your e-mail signature at the bottom of your pitch, include your name, contact info, titles (with hyperlinks to any external websites like Amazon or your corporate site), and any other important info.

Why should contact info come at the end? Because most of the media will respond back to your e-mail if they're interested. Your contact info and "sale" aren't important elements to them. They know why you're contacting them in the first place.

Notice I said nothing about selling your product or service. It's only about selling your expertise and the quality of insight and analysis you can provide.

The last thing a content producer wants to do is run a free commercial for you or your business. That's boring and not newsworthy... unless you're a famous CEO of a reputable company or something in that league.

How To Write And Submit A Press Release

Consider submitting a press release for anything newsworthy.

As a business owner or marketer, your newsworthy stories could be:

- Raising a round of funding

- Appointing a big name to your management team or board of directors

- Launching a new product

- Reporting earnings

- Acquiring a new company

Taking the elements from your pitch, you can tie in the newsworthy parts into a proper press release format. The subject line can be your title. You can Google "press release template" to see what the format looks like and go off it. I'm also pasting a sample press release I did for a client at the end of this section so you can see the format in real-time.

To submit your press release to the wires without having to pay hundreds of dollars on a subscription, go to www.fiverr.com or www.upwork.com (formerly Elance/oDesk) and enter the search terms "Newswire" or "PR Newswire." Sort the results by rating, and hire someone with five-star reviews to submit your press release through the wires.

There are numerous press wires available – both free and paid – but Newswire services have the best connection to Google. They do a good job of getting your press release on Google News, leading to the release rising to the top of Google search. They also distribute your release to leading publications like the *Miami Herald*, *Boston Globe*, and *Digital Journal*.

Sample Press Release Format

[Full Date]

FOR IMMEDIATE RELEASE

[Enticing Title] (similar to subject line of pitch)

[City, State] – Leading Wall Street real estate note firm Watermark Trading Exchange (http://www.WatermarkExchange.com) [hyperlink to your site and also write out the full URL because some wires will strip hyperlinks] announced today that it has added the option for buyers to transact in bitcoin. Previously, users could only make purchases in U.S. dollars or euros.

Watermark Exchange will be the first trading company in United States to accept bitcoin for note sales.

"We understand bitcoin is becoming a very important way of paying for transactions, so we've been working hard to integrate bitcoin capabilities into our platform," Founder & CEO of Watermark Trading Exchange Val Sotir said. "Our team is constantly looking for ways to improve the trading experience of our clients. We really believe that adding bitcoin as a form of payment on our exchange will offer even more flexibility to our international real estate investors looking to add defaulted notes to their own portfolio."

Sotir, a 23-year Wall Street veteran in the trading and mortgage industry, said his firm has gotten numerous inquiries from international investors – particularly from Europe, South America and Asia – about being able to accept bitcoin. Watermark's entry into the digital currency space gives buyers more flexibility to pay.

Watermark has a designated trading desk to convert bitcoin payments directly into U.S. dollars, and it has retained BitPay as its payment processor. This move was meant to ensure Watermark could serve a larger section of the US investor market.

Bitcoin and digital currencies burst into the mainstream in 2013, and they have become a topic of great debate by politicians, regulators, retail owners, and financial professionals.

About Watermark Trading Exchange

Watermark Trading Exchange connects Wall Street institutional mortgage wholesalers with Main Street retail note buyers who are usually only able to obtain notes privately on a one-off basis. Watermark Exchange is accommodating banks, larger hedge funds and private equity firms to sell their portfolios, creating liquidity so investors can buy more loans at much better pricing.

Watermark Trading Exchange has hundreds of assets for sale across the United States for investors to purchase.

For more information about the Watermark Trading Exchange, visit its official website at www.watermarkexchange.com.

For questions, comments or media inquiries, contact Val Sotir at [enter e-mail] or [enter phone].

Media Contact:

[enter full name]

[enter e-mail]

[enter phone]

###

Categories and keyword/tags: real estate, mortgage, notes, bonds, institutions, trading, Wall Street, finance, digital currency, investing, banking, investments, computer science, technology, education, economics, bitcoin

How To Hire A Publicist If You're Too Busy To Do Your Own PR

If you have no time to do your own publicity, then what should you do?

Find independent publicists on www.upwork.com (formerly Elance/oDesk). Work out a tiered payment structure with a small PR firm (one or two person shop) so you **pay per booking**. If you struggle to find someone you like, then contact me at naresh dot vissa at gmail dot com, and I'll connect you with an honest and small PR shop that can get you the visibility you need at the right prices.

Here's an example of a tiered structure:

> **Tier 1**: top 50 ranking podcasts on iTunes, newsletter podcasts, newsletter interviews and features, pubs with dogmatic followings, mainstream media: like CNBC, FOX, CNN, etc.
> Price: $150/booking
>
> **Tier 2**: niche mainstream media: RT, Al Jazeera, CCTV, and relevant print pubs
> Price: $100/booking
>
> **Tier 3**: smaller online publications: TheStreet, big blogs, etc.
> Price: $50/booking

Tier 4: small blogs and podcasts, BlogTalk Radio, terrestrial radio
Price: $40/booking

A tiered structure allows the PR firm to charge for performance (per booking), and the client knows exactly what he or she is getting and paying for. You both can decide the tiers and what criteria constitute each one. In this type of arrangement, the chances of anyone being scammed or shortchanged is near none.

5 Ways To Do Media Interviews

Historically, reporters and interviewees have preferred to conduct face-to-face interviews. That is changing. Interviews can now be conducted via e-mail, phone, Skype, or Google Hangouts. Be ready to give interviews through all these media.

1) Skype

For video, radio, or podcast interviews, use Skype. The sound quality on Skype audio is much greater than landline or cell phone.

If the host of a show doesn't do Skype interviews, then that's a sign that the show has a small following and they're not running their production correctly. The sound quality of the show could be low, which means the production team doesn't know what it's doing.

This is not a good way to conduct or run a business.

For audio interviews, use a good microphone. Here are some recommendations:

Mac users – Blue Microphone's Snowball USB and iRig… these microphones have some of the best sound quality on the market.

Cost: about $55

Windows users – Audio Technica… there are various versions of this mic. Generally, the more expensive the Audio Technica, the better the quality.

Cost: You can get a very high quality Audio Technica mic for less than $40.

USE A FOAM WINDSCREEN to capture and filter sound. Windscreens reduce the occurrence of wind, breath sounds and popping noises. They keep mics clean and extend their lifetimes. Most windscreens fit standard microphones.

Cost: $5

To buy equipment, USE AMAZON. Amazon is the one of the best online marketplaces on the Internet. The prices of products these days are INCREDIBLE… thanks to Amazon!

NOTE: DO NOT USE THE BUILT-IN MICROPHONE IN YOUR COMPUTER. Built-in mics are okay for casual use, but for professional quality, you'll want to invest in one of the microphones I mentioned.

2) Google Hangouts

Some up-and-coming, newer video shows will want to do interviews on Google Hangouts. Google Hangouts has even better functionalities than Skype. You can video chat with multiple users, insert computerized graphics, and record conversations.

All you need to use Google Hangouts is a Gmail account. You can use your computer's built-in microphone and camera because an external microphone or headset will be distracting to viewers.

3) Landline Telephone

If you're on a radio show or podcast that doesn't conduct Skype audio interviews, then your next option should be landline telephone. Landlines have better quality than cell phones.

4) Cell Phone

For print interviews with a newspaper, magazine, or blog, cell phone is OK.

5) E-mail

E-mail interviews are popular, but they benefit the reporter or writer more than the source because it takes a long time to draft a thorough e-mail with quality content. What you write in e-mail becomes your facts. You can't clarify whatever you say in the future.

How To Keep Track Of Media Mentions

What happens if the media or Internet sphere references you without your knowledge? First, that's a good sign. It means you're doing something right for the media to mention you or your work without your knowledge. You're getting free publicity without even trying!

The easiest way to track this is by creating Google Alerts for your name. Doing so is simple… go to www.google.com/alerts, and set an alert for your name or product in quotations. "Naresh Vissa" would be my alert. You can set as many alerts as you'd like. So if you're the marketing director of a company with several executives and quality brands or products, you can track all online buzz by creating Google Alerts for each item's name.

Why Getting On Wikipedia Is The Ultimate PR Stamp

The end goal with getting all the media attention I laid out: getting a Wikipedia entry. But it's not so easy.

Wikipedia is now *the* go-to for research. Its search engine optimization (SEO) is one of the best – meaning Google usually ranks Wikipedia entries on the first page of a search query.

The WikiPolice consists of thousands of volunteers worldwide who monitor Wikipedia activity. If you try to publish a Wikipedia on yourself or your company, the WikiPolice will shut it down if it doesn't meet the Wikipedia standards.

There used to be a PR firm called Wiki-PR, which wrote Wikipedia entries for clients, but Wikipedia banned it for writing entries that weren't worthy enough.

My recommendation: get yourself as much PR as possible so that someone else (maybe even a WikiPolice member) can create a Wikipedia entry for you. Once you get your own Wikipedia page created, that's when you know you made it – for better or for worse.

Chapter 26:
HOW MILLENNIAL MARKETING
WILL GET YOU GEN Y CUSTOMERS

Millennials are the future consumers of the world. I say *future* because millennials are still young enough to be trying to earn a living to spend money on luxury goods that companies can market.

According to the *Merriam-Webster Dictionary*, a millennial is "a person born in the 1980s or 1990s."

In other words, a millennial is a person who reached or will reach young adulthood around the year 2000 or later. Millennials are under 40-years-old and are a part of Generation Y, hence why people refer to them as Gen Y'ers.

I'm a millennial since I was born in the 1980's. My experience has taught me a little bit about marketing as a producer and consumer.

Millennials are the largest Generation in U.S. history, says the National Conference on Citizenship. There are now more than 80 million millennials – larger than the Baby Boomers and more than twice the size of Generation X.

Many small business owners should be interested in millennial spending habits. Bar and club owners, tech and gadget entrepreneurs and content publishers are just a few individuals who should care about marketing to millennials.

Millennials may not have all the money in the world saved up in their bank accounts, but they're still very much interested in purchasing products. Accenture estimates they spend more than $600 billion a year – the largest of any living segment.

There's an even later Generation to Gen Y: Gen Z. These are folks born in the 90's. Most research firms still couple anyone born after the 80's (including 90's babies) as Gen Y.

Gen Y/Gen Z is prominent in online spend. As these Generations mature, the spending can only go up.

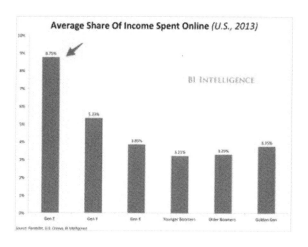

So, as a marketer, how can you resonate with the millennials?

It's all about *branding*. I've spoken at length throughout this book about the importance of directly reaching your target consumer, and you still need to do that with millennials. Don't treat this chapter as the only information you need to know to reach millennials. The other principles and strategies are just as important.

With millennials, in addition, you must create a brand for yourself and display it digitally, particularly through social media and mobile. Millennials like their phones, iPads, and MacBooks. They now do everything on it... watch TV, read books on iBooks or Kindle and articles on Twitter, stalk on Facebook, Skype or FaceTime with their family. Because they do so much digitally, viewing a brand through these media holds more strength than viewing a brand on a billboard or in a magazine. Millennials likely won't even get to see these types of ads or brands because they're moving away from consuming content in this manner.

So this means, to start, you have to:

- Create a Facebook Fan Page

- Run Facebook ads to your target market

- Create a Twitter handle

- Create Instagram and Pinterest accounts and post pictures of your products

- Create a Google+ page

- Create a LinkedIn Company Page

- Create a YouTube channel

- Create a Tumblr

- Create a Snapchat account

- Create a Myspace account

- Release content on all your social media frequently to build up and engage with followers

- Pump out good content on your site and disseminate it through your social media and mailing list

- Pump out good content on other sites to establish your authority and increase your "popularity"

HubSpot found that millennial users are 71% more likely to purchase a product based on social media referrals. Social media is *social...* not commercial. But a recommendation from a friend is a lot more powerful than an ad on TV. Social media are set up so that people can post their thoughts in an open forum… and their "friends" have access to this information and can decide what to do with it and if they should act on it.

Despite teens publicly hating on Facebook, Forrester Research found that they are still using it more than any other social media network.

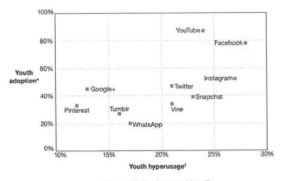

Piper Jaffray also found that Instagram is quickly becoming a go-to network among teens. That's not surprising, given that Facebook owns Instagram. Instagram isn't the most widely used with teens, but surveys have revealed that teens like it the best out of all the other social networks and apps.

Nielsen found that YouTube attracts more millennials to its site than any TV channel on cable. *Business Insider* reported that YouTube is now the one-stop destination for millennials to consume visual content, ahead of ESPN and Comedy Central.

People still want to be engaged in meaningful ways, but they must be different ways from the past.

Millennials Want Quick & Easy

The digital age has coincided with millennial maturation. Millennial men don't want to shop at department or grocery stores anymore. Retails shop customers are slowly becoming predominantly female.

Bank branches have less millennial customers visiting them because millennials would rather deposit their checks or make changes to their accounts online or through their mobile phones.

Millennials are now moving money at a rapid rate among millennials through payment processors like Square and payment transmitters like PayPal and Venmo. The big banks are also improving their own applications to improve commerce, which the millennials are making use of.

Spanish is the second most spoken language in the United States. Media Metrix Multi-Platform found that two out of every five millennials of Spanish-speaking origin are "mobile-only" users – meaning they don't use computers or tablets for anything. They conduct all their business – reading, communicating, working – on their phones.

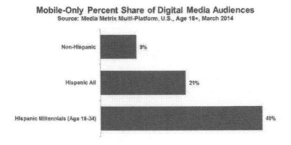

Media Metrix Multi-Platform found that one out of every five American millennials is "mobile-only."

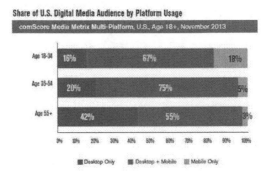

And the adoption of smartphones among millennials has surpassed any other age class. This is despite millennials not having as much money in the bank as their older counterparts, who are more likely to afford intricate smartphones and their data plans.

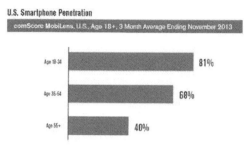

U.S. Smartphone Penetration

comScore MobiLens, U.S., Age 18+, 3 Month Average Ending November 2013

Age 18-34: 81%
Age 35-54: 68%
Age 55+: 40%

Millennials have grown up in a changing – and improving – technological environment. The Internet was big in the 90's, and then iPods and laptops ruled the first decade of the 2000's. Now, tablets and mobile are dominating the second decade of the 2000's. That's why millennials are quick adopters and better adapters. There wasn't so much technological change during the Baby Boomer days.

Importance Of Reputation

The digital environment gives users access to vet any company or product. A negative reputation can have an enormous impact on a business.

For example, if you're a restaurant and you have lousy Yelp reviews, or even a couple of bad Yelp reviews, then people will actually make their decisions not to eat at your restaurant based on those reviews.

The same can be said about Amazon reviews for authors, Better Business Review ratings for consumer businesses, negative blog posts, Tweets, Facebook Graph Searches, etc.

Millennial Marketing Wrap-up

Having a digital presence may not increase your sales immediately, but it will keep millennials from shutting you out altogether because you're stuck in the Dark Ages.

When I was in graduate school at Duke University's Fuqua School of Business, a successful publishing company recruited me to run a new media division. The company sold themselves as being so big and successful, but I didn't believe it because they had ZERO presence in digital. I couldn't find any positive media done on them. There weren't many employees listed on LinkedIn. And their website looked like it was created in the mid-90's.

At the time, I was 23 and planned to work on Wall Street, so this was a huge step down from what I wanted. I wrote the publishing company off and had no intention of working for them. But they really wanted me, so I finally gave them one shot at an interview. After conducting months of due diligence, I found no red flags. This company simply had no digital presence.

As a company in the digital age, you don't want recruits or potential customers shutting you out before they even *try* you.

Chapter 27:
HOW TO INCORPORATE GENDER MARKETING

Women control household spending. Whether it's through their own bank accounts or telling their significant others what to do with their money, women account for 80% of household spending in some way, shape or form, according to TechCrunch.

Women like to shop, but when it comes to online and digital shopping, women are not as interested as men are. Men have now surpassed women in shopping spend in the digital world, as reported by the *Huffington Post*. I'm not sure why. Maybe men are more tech savvy than women. That should explain why so many computer programmers are male... and why tech firms in Silicon Valley get a lot of heat for not having enough women.

Regardless, this means *something* to marketers in the digital world. It doesn't mean that all of your buyers will be male... but it does mean that, if you're a generic, gender-neutral business – like a restaurant or gym or airline – more of your digital traffic will be coming from males. Keep this in mind when formulating your designs, development and marketing campaigns.

What does that mean?

- **Colors**: you'll want to stick to standard colors – not hot pink or purple

- **Images**: again, standard images – nothing too cheesy or romantic

- **Tone**: the copy should be straightforward... no need to throw in sharp emotion

Of course, if you're a lingerie retailer or feminist publisher, then almost all of your traffic will be female, so you can plan accordingly for that.

There really isn't much more to gender marketing. Once you know your demographic, you'll know how to tailor your message because your audience will *tell you how* they want to be sold.

So listen to them.

Chapter 28:
HOW TO BRAND YOURSELF FOR DIGITAL DISCOVERY TO MAKE YOUR DREAMS COME TRUE

I know of countless people who give up their lives to start anew... not because they want to, but because they think they have to. Here's what I mean...

A friend of mine moved to LA so he could network with entertainment agents.

Another friend moved to the Valley to find a job at a start-up.

And someone else moved out of the United States to live alone for a year to write a book.

The greatness of the new, digital age is remoteness. Physical presence and labor is a dying breed. Cheaper, more productive digital workflows are slashing in-person contact.

This is all for the better... and here's how you can benefit...

If you want to become a comedian or singer or dancer or any other type of performer, then create a

YouTube channel so the world can tune in. That's what Justin Bieber did when he was a sane little boy. After his first hit release, "Baby," he became the most viewed male artist on YouTube, which then propelled him to the mainstream.

If you want to make movies, then use your iPhone to shoot video. The iPhone 6s has a better camera than the 90% of the cameras priced below $3,000. My old iPhone 4s had a better camera than the cameras Syracuse University provided me in journalism school. You can then upload your masterpiece that was taken on your phone to YouTube and submit it to Amazon Studios so the world can view it. My friend Aneesh Chaganty shot a short on Google Glass. His two-minute film ("Seeds") is on YouTube. It has more than three million views.

If you want to become a screenwriter, then upload your screenplays to Amazon Studios, Scribd, and Black List. Hollywood producers are always checking these sites for ideas.

If you want to become an author, then self-publish your books on Amazon. That's what Fifty Shades of Grey author E.L. James did. She's sold more than 150 million copies of her books, which are also being adapted into movies.

If you want to become a broadcaster or commentator, then start a podcast and distribute it

240

through iTunes, TuneIn, Stitcher, and SoundCloud. That's what John Lee Dumas did. He has tens of millions of listeners worldwide and makes millions of dollars every year through his podcasting products.

If you want to start a business, then set up a "home office" with your cell phone, laptop, and Skype. You have everything you need to get started. That's what I did when I went out on my own. I've started at least five businesses since then.

If you're looking for a job, then create your digital resume on LinkedIn. That's how I got my first full-time job after school. Someone found me on LinkedIn and then hired me a few hours later. It was that quick.

If you're looking for a job, then network online with companies in the closest big city to you. Many companies – large and small – have presences in under-the-radar cities like Tampa, Memphis, Wilmington (Delaware), Jacksonville, and Salt Lake City. Hiring managers in these cities are tired of recruiting from the local state school and are screaming for more talent. Location isn't an issue anymore.

Gone are the days of moving to LA to make it in Hollywood...

Or moving to the Valley to start a business...

Or to New York City to find a job...

The only day is now. There are no more excuses.

The world as we know it is improving day-by-day. Processes are becoming more efficient, and the cream is finding quicker, newer ways to rise to the top of the crop.

Don't be left behind.

RESOURCES

I laid out a lot of material in the book. It's impossible to remember everything. So I'll lay out the "smaller picture" resources you can use.

These resources are websites, apps, products and services to improve your marketing efforts. They are not big picture tools like Facebook, Instagram, and WordPress. Those resources have entire chapters dedicated to them and are referenced throughout the book.

Outsourcing Tasks (design/development, monotonous labor, skilled labor, etc.)

www.fiverr.com

www.upwork.com

Mailing List

www.MailChimp.com – Easy-to-use e-mail service provider (ESP) that is quality and cheaper compared to competitors like AWeber, Constant Contact, iContact and Infusionsoft.

Affiliates

www.similarsites.com – Search for and research potential affiliates in your niche.

www.mixpanel.com – Analytics platform offers a variety of free and paid products and services, including the creation of affiliate links and tracking clicks, orders, leads and referrals.

www.clickbank.com – Most popular affiliate marketing outlet because it's been around since the late 90's.

Shopping Cart

www.nanacast.com – Shopping cart includes affiliate services, instant revenue sharing, one-click upsells, and integrates into all e-mail service providers.

Customer Lifetime Value

www.customerlifetimevalue.co – Free customer lifetime value calculator for your business or product.

Social Media

www.hootsuite.com – Social media management dashboard where users can manage all their accounts through a centralized platform. Instead of manually posting on every one of your social media accounts individually, connect your accounts to Hootsuite and send messages out to all your networks with one post and mouse click.

www.Tweriod.com – See when your Twitter followers are most active.

Social sharing buttons on posts – Plugin for WordPress with little sharing icons above or below articles... having them encourages readers to share content with their networks.

Advertising

www.whatrunswhere.com – Provides detailed intelligence on what and where your competition is advertising. This is the perfect way to pay for your competition's inside information and secrets!

Landing Pages

www.leadpages.net – Gives designed templates for landing pages of all kinds: lead generation, squeeze pages, order forms (long and short), shopping carts, webinars, and more. If you don't want to pay a web designer or developer for thousands of dollars a month, then LeadPages is your solution... for the low cost of $40 a month with the Pro Annual package (which I recommend over the $25 Standard package, which doesn't come with as many useful features).

Syndication

Content:

- *Huffington Post*

- *Medium*

- LinkedIn

- Facebook status/Fan Page

- Publishers/blogs (big and small) in your niche

- Guest Post Articles (www.guestpostarticles.com) – marketplace that helps match guest bloggers, article writers, and marketers with blogs and website publishers who want guest posts, articles, and reviews

Podcasts:

- iTunes

- TuneIn (www.tunein.com)

- Stitcher (www.stitcher.com)

- SoundCloud (www.soundcloud.com)

- Player FM (www.player.fm)

- Spreaker (www.spreaker.com)

- Many other smaller distributors (you can get a full list by purchasing my previous book PODCASTNOMICS: The Book Of

Podcasting... To Make You Millions on Amazon)

eBooks (Amazon):

-   KDP (Kindle)

-   CreateSpace (Paperback)

-   Audible (Audiobook)

-   Smashwords (iBooks)

Slide decks – SlideShare (www.slideshare.com)

Videos – YouTube

Webinars – YouTube

Reviews – www.productsforreview.com allows marketers to get reviews of their products. For $10, submit a product for review, and the site will send your query out to a broad list of potential reviewers, who will contact you for a sample if they're interested.

Book Self-Publishing

www.createspace.com – Publish a paperback and Kindle e-book to Amazon.

kdp.amazon.com – Publish a Kindle e-book to Amazon.

www.acx.com – Find someone to narrate your audiobook and then publish it to Amazon.

YouTube Video

www.ShareYouTubeVideos.com – Buy views, likes, shares and more for your YouTube video.

Webinars

www.techsmith.com/camtasia – Record yourself giving your webinar presentation FREE for 30 days. Camtasia connects directly to PowerPoint and allows you to edit at the end.

www.instanttelesimar.com – Webinar software allows subscribers to integrate their marketing with solid lead generation and customer service.

PR

www.helpareporter.com – Become a source by getting expert requests from media and journalists delivered straight to your e-mail inbox.

www.RadioGuestList.com – Similar to Help A Reporter, Radio Guest List sends one e-mail every two days, and it only sends out radio and podcast queries.

www.google.com/alerts – Easiest way to track your online mentions in real-time.

MICROPHONES:

Mac users – Blue Microphone's Snowball USB and iRig

Windows users – Audio Technica

Books

Surprisingly, there aren't many up-to-date marketing handbooks that provide actionable guidance AND macro research on trends. Too many books focus on only one marketing channel (like just YouTube or just Facebook or just lead-generation) or spin their strategies into dreamy "get rich quick" schemes.

I've read (and written ;-) through the noise and found the best books that provide great roadmaps on digital marketing principles:

TRACTION: How Any Startup Can Achieve Explosive Customer Growth (2015 edition or later) by Gabriel Weinberg and Justin Mares

THE NEW RULES OF MARKETING & PR: How to Use Social Media, Online Video, Mobile Applications, Blogs, News Releases, and Viral Marketing to Reach Buyers Directly (2015 edition or later) by David Meerman Scott

THE LONG TAIL: Why the Future of Business is Selling Less of More by Chris Anderson (though this came out in 2008, the principles are timeless)

<u>PODCASTNOMICS: The Book Of Podcasting… To Make You Millions</u> by Naresh Vissa

If you need any online/digital marketing or project management services performed, then e-mail me at naresh dot Vissa at Gmail dot com and my firm, Krish Media & Marketing, should have solutions for you. I'm also glad to answer any questions you have to point you in the right direction.

STAY IN TOUCH

Tweet me @xnareshx.

Visit www.nareshvissa.com to subscribe to my FREE newsletter mailing list.

For a full list of services my marketing agency, Krish Media & Marketing, offers, visit www.krishmediamarketing.com.

If you have any questions or would like some online marketing or project management services, e-mail me at naresh dot vissa @ gmail dot com.

Please leave a review of this book on Amazon!

REFERENCES

"18-34 Year Olds Are Watching 53% More Online Video [Study]." *ReelSEO*. 08 Sept. 2014.

"71% More Likely to Purchase Based on Social Media Referrals [Infographic]." *71% More Likely to Purchase Based on Social Media Referrals [Infographic]*.

"Ad Agencies See Effectiveness in Online Video - EMarketer." *Ad Agencies See Effectiveness in Online Video - EMarketer*.

"The Best and Worst Times to Post on Social Networks (Infographic)." *Social Media Consultant Social Media Agency Social Marketing RSS*. 18 July 2012.

"Borders Files for Bankruptcy." *DealBook Borders Files for Bankruptcy*. 16 Feb. 2011.

"Boring Landing Pages Increase Sales and Conversions." *EMarketing & Commerce (eM+C)*.

"Business Insider Raises New Round; Valued at $100 Mln -source." *Reuters*. Thomson Reuters, 05 Mar. 2014.

"Business Insider Sold to German Media Giant." *Fortune Business Insider Sold at 442 Million Valuation Comments.* 29 Sept. 2015.

Clifford, Stephanie. "Stuff Piled in the Aisle? It's There to Get You to Spend More." *The New York Times.* The New York Times, 07 Apr. 2011.

"The Complete Follow-Up Email Frequency Guide." *Yesware Blog The Complete Sales Email Frequency Guide Why It Pays To FollowUp Comments.* 19 Nov. 2014.

Danova, Tony. "How Often Should I Update My App? Businesses Should Consider The Benefits Of Frequent App Updates." *Business Insider.* Business Insider, Inc, 16 Jan. 2015.

"Despite Losing Its Cool, Facebook Is Still The Most Popular Social Network For Teens." *Fast Company.* 24 June 2014.

"Domino's Pizza Gets Flirty on Tinder for Valentine's Day." *Domino's Pizza Gets Flirty on Tinder for Valentine's Day.*

"End of the Book for Barnes and Noble?" *WND.*

"Facebook Most Used Mobile App, Google App 10th." *Marketing Land.* 04 Dec. 2013.

"Gartner Says Worldwide PC, Tablet and Mobile Phone Combined Shipments to Reach 2.4 Billion Units in 2013." *Gartner Says Worldwide PC, Tablet and Mobile Phone Combined Shipments to Reach 2.4 Billion Units in 2013.*

Green, Joshua. "The Science Behind Those Obama Campaign E-Mails." *Bloomberg Business Week.* Bloomberg, 29 Nov. 2012.

"How the New Right Hand Column Ads Are Delivering Greater Value." *Facebook for Business.*

"How to Advertise on a Porn Website | Eat24 Blog." *Bacon Sriracha Unicorn Diaries.* 09 Sept. 2013.

"IBM 2012 Holiday Benchmark Reports." *IBM 2012 Holiday Benchmark Reports.*

"Infographic: India to Become the Third Largest Smartphone Market by 2017." *Statista Infographics.*

"Is Bigger Better? Mobile Marketers Right-size Their Efforts." - *Mobile Marketer.*

"Just How Big Are Porn Sites? | ExtremeTech." *ExtremeTech.*

"Killers of Craigslist." *Law Street (TM).* 28 Oct. 2014.

Kleinman, Alexis. "Porn Sites Get More Visitors Each Month Than Netflix, Amazon And Twitter Combined." *The Huffington Post.* TheHuffingtonPost.com.

Krupnick, Ellie. "Men's Online Shopping Surpasses Women's (INFOGRAPHIC)." *The Huffington Post.* TheHuffingtonPost.com.

"LSA|14: Gian Fulgoni, Executive Chairman and Co-Founder, ComScore." *LSA|14: Gian Fulgoni, Executive Chairman and Co-Founder, ComScore.*

"Medialets Mobile & Tablet Advertising Benchmarks: H1-2014." *Medialets.* 12 Aug. 2014.

"Meet The Mobile App Install Addict." *12/17/2014.*

"Native Ad Research from IPG & Sharethrough Reveals That In-Feed Beats Banners - Sharethrough." *Sharethrough.*

"NCoC: Two Special Generations: The Millennials and the Boomers." *NCoC: Two Special Generations: The Millennials and the Boomers.*

"New Facebook Rules Will Sting Entrepreneurs." *WSJ.*

"News Apps Have Longest Life, Games, The Shortest." *02/21/2014.*

"The NY Times Is Going Bankrupt – LewRockwell.com." *LewRockwell.*

"Report: We Now Spend More Time On Mobile Devices Than TV." *Marketing Land.* 18 Nov. 2014.

"Reports." *An Era of Growth: The Cross-Platform Report Q4 2013.*

Roche, Julia La. "Greg Smith Just Got A $1.5 Million Advance For His Goldman Sachs Tell-All." *Business Insider.* Business Insider, Inc, 30 Mar. 2012.

"Smartphone Users in the U.S. 2010-2018 | Forecast." *Statista.*

"Social Media for the Productivity Win - HootSuite Social Media." *Hootsuite Social Media Management.* 15 Apr. 2013.

"State of the U.S. Online Retail Economy in Q1 2014." *ComScore, Inc.*

"Study: 30% of People Are on Social Media at Work for One Hour Everyday." *Social Media Today.* 10 May 2013.

"Study: Online Shopping Behavior in the Digital Era | IAcquire Blog." *IAcquire Study Online Shopping Behavior in the Digital Era Comments.*

"Taking Stock With Teens - Fall 2014." *Taking Stock With Teens - Fall 2014.*

"TIL Reddit Users Donated $185,356.70 to Direct Relief International for Haiti after the Earthquake Devastated the Island in January, 2010. • /r/reddit.com." *Reddit.*

"Top Sites." *Alexa.*

"Two Out of Five Hispanic Millennials Are Mobile-Only Internet Users." *ComScore, Inc.*

"Why Women Rule The Internet." *TechCrunch.*

"YouTube Reaches More Young Viewers than Any Cable Network, Says Nielsen." *SlashGear.* 01 May 2013.

Made in the USA
Charleston, SC
30 December 2015